"Navigating the teen years is a c[...] thoughtful, well-informed, and easy-to-read guide can help you under-stand how anxiety works, what makes it better, and what makes it worse. With a logical and systematic road map based in scientific research and clinical expertise, you can use effective strategies to support and coach your teen through anxiety, stress, and worry. A must-read!"

—**Aureen Wagner, PhD**, adjunct associate professor at the University of North Carolina at Chapel Hill, director at The Anxiety Wellness Center, and author of *Worried No More*

"A wonderful addition to the self-help literature, *Helping Your Anxious Teen* details a specific, pragmatic action plan for parents of 13–19 year olds. The delicate balance of supporting teens emotionally without enabling their anxiety is nicely described, as is the way to teach skills without taking over. Worry, perfectionism, panic, and fear—this book covers anxiety in its many forms, bringing hope and, even more to the point, *relief* to struggling parents and teens."

—**Dawn Huebner, PhD**, psychologist and author of *What to Do When You Worry Too Much*

"*Helping Your Anxious Teen* is an excellent resource for parents search-ing for thoughtful and effective strategies to effectively parent their anxious teen. The book is filled with useful advice and proven-effective techniques parents can use to guide their anxious teen through a criti-cal time in their development."

—**Michael A. Tompkins, PhD**, codirector of the San Francisco Bay Area Center for Cognitive Therapy; assistant clinical professor at the University of California, Berkeley; and coauthor of *My Anxious Mind*

"Sheila Achar Josephs will teach you how to coach your teen to develop the valuable skills that can lead them toward a more flexible—and independent—path into adulthood."

—**Reid Wilson, PhD**, coauthor of *Anxious Kids, Anxious Parents*

"*Helping Your Anxious Teen* makes a valuable and impressive contribution by providing a clear, effective, and easy-to-read guide for parents to help their adolescent overcome anxiety. Chapters describe the nature of anxiety, how to understand its presentation, and, perhaps most importantly, how parents can help their teen conquer fear and stress. This book is a must-have for any parent of an anxious teen, as well as for providers who work with this population."

—**Eric Storch, PhD**, All Children's Hospital Guild Endowed Chair and Professor at the University of South Florida, and clinical director at Rogers Behavioral Health-Tampa Bay

"Anxiety is a cage that locks teens in, preventing them from fully engaging in life. Sheila Achar Josephs is a master clinician who gives parents the keys to help teens break free of fear-filled suffering and constraints."

—**Eileen Kennedy-Moore, PhD**, coauthor of *Smart Parenting for Smart Kids*

"This terrific book puts the time-tested and research-proven strategies of cognitive behavioral therapy (CBT) into a very readable format that will help you be a more effective coach and cheerleader when it comes to parenting your own anxious or stressed-out teen. You will find the numerous illustrative examples and step-by-step instructions for implementing the techniques extremely helpful. Every parent should read this book!"

—**Jonathan Abramowitz, PhD**, director of the Anxiety and Stress Disorders Clinic at University of North Carolina at Chapel Hill

Helping Your *Anxious* Teen

Positive Parenting Strategies to Help Your
Teen Beat Anxiety, Stress, and Worry

SHEILA ACHAR JOSEPHS, PhD

New Harbinger Publications, Inc.

Publisher's Note

Distributed in Canada by Raincoast Books

Copyright © 2016 by Sheila Achar Josephs
        New Harbinger Publications, Inc.
        5674 Shattuck Avenue
        Oakland, CA 94609
        www.newharbinger.com

Cover design by Amy Shoup

Acquired by Wendy Millstine

Edited by Kristi Hein

FSC
www.fsc.org
MIX
Paper from
responsible sources
FSC® C011935

Library of Congress Cataloging-in-Publication Data on file

18   17   16

10   9   8   7   6   5   4   3   2   1   First Printing

This book is dedicated to my mother, Malathi Achar, for her wisdom and loving support, and to my father, Dr. B. R. Achar, who taught me to dream big. It is also dedicated to the children and teens I have worked with over the years, who, with the help of their parents, bravely pushed themselves to face their fears, and discovered freedom from anxiety.

Contents

Note to the Reader

The vignettes in this book are fictional and based on a composite of teens and their families rather than specific people or events. Any identifying information has been changed or removed. This book is for general educational purposes only and does not represent individual professional advice nor the provision of psychological services. Appendix D is a list of associations that provide education and support to families.

Reader comments are welcome. For readers interested in commenting on the book, signing up for a future newsletter, or seeking psychological services, visit http://www.sheilaacharjosephs.com or http://www.princetoncognitivetherapy.com.

Introduction

Anxiety suddenly hit my teen like a tsunami wave. Some days were fine, but on others, she seemed really worried. She even started to avoid situations that made her anxious. I tried to give her encouragement but couldn't get through to her. Before we knew it, we were all on edge. Anxiety had moved into our home and become the boss.

—Parent of an anxious teen

As a parent of an anxious teen, you know how strong anxiety's grip on your teen can be. You can see it on your teen's face—the tension and worry. You notice how your teen's behavior has changed. You wish she could just brush off her fears and focus on the positive things in her life, and yet it is not so easy. Anxiety's footprint is large.

You may have a daughter mired in worry or a son who avoids social situations. Maybe you have a teen who gets really worked up about doing perfectly at school. Perhaps you have a daughter who panics in certain situations or a son who gets stressed out over every little thing. Regardless of the particular way that anxiety takes hold, you share a burden with other parents of anxious children: witnessing anxiety's strong impact on your child and your family. Anxiety takes what might have been a normal day or week and turns it topsy-turvy. Now everyone seems to be at anxiety's beck and call. And sometimes your teen is just miserable. You may wonder at this point: *Where did my happy child go?*

Parenting an anxious teen is a real challenge. You try to help your teen feel better and encourage him to let go of his fears, but the more you try, the more he tells you that you don't understand. You reason with him when he is caught up in worry, but more often than not your reasoning seems to go unheard. You give your teen advice on how to solve a problem, but he won't listen to you. When you see him avoid a challenge, you describe the ways that facing it won't be so bad; yet despite all of your efforts, your teen remains stuck in the throes of fear, worry, and avoidance.

It is not surprising that anxious teens are so challenging to support. Adolescence itself, with its developmental changes and increased stress, has a formidable impact on teens. During this time, many triggers of anxiety all interact with one another. On top of that, the strategies for reducing anxiety can seem very counterintuitive. For example, to reduce anxiety, you may first have to deliberately increase it. All in all, there are good reasons why anxiety remains stuck despite every parent's best efforts to reduce it.

When perfectly logical attempts by parents to help their teens don't work, they ask, "Why isn't my approach working?" and "How do I get through to my teen when she is so anxious?" I wrote this book to answer such questions. And the good news is that parents can do a lot to help their teens fight anxiety. Despite how stuck your teen might seem right now, given the right tools, teens can overcome their anxiety. Indeed, there really is light at the end of the tunnel!

Over the past twenty years, I have been privileged in my work as a psychologist and anxiety specialist to help teens overcome their anxiety and live fulfilling lives. When anxiety lifts, a huge burden is released. For example, a thirteen-year-old boy who had recently overcome his anxiety happily grinned at me and said, "Life is goooood." It felt so wonderfully freeing to him to finally feel better! I have successfully used powerful methods, which I discuss in this book, to treat teens, preteens, and younger children with all types of anxiety problems, from worries to social anxiety, panic, and obsessive-compulsive symptoms. Maladaptive anxiety, the kind that really gets in the way, can be reduced and often removed altogether.

Parents Are a Key to Success

In the process of helping teens, I learned long ago that involving parents in the journey of change is critical to having a lasting and powerful impact on reducing anxiety. I then began guiding parents to successfully team up with their teens to reduce anxiety. These parents excitedly discovered that by applying the strategies discussed in this book, they can indeed spark positive shifts in their teen's mood and behavior. They learn to function as behind-the-scenes coaches, gently guiding their teen toward reduced distress. My teen clients also appreciated that their parents better understood anxiety and had learned to gently redirect them when it loomed large.

Serving as a coach to help your teen reduce anxiety has multiple benefits. It allows you to closely partner with your teen to defeat anxiety, rather than allowing it to get between the two of you. With your coaching you can foster motivation and effort by providing encouragement and inspiration as well as ample praise and reinforcement for brave behavior. Like any good coach, you can identify the weaknesses of your opponent—in this case, anxiety—and your teen's strengths to overcome it. Lastly, you can (1) remind your teen to practice the strategies described in this book, (2) demonstrate how to do the strategies, and (3) push your teen to persevere through tough times.

Research backs up the value of including parents in the treatment of adolescents; it increases treatment effectiveness and, even more important, gives positive gains more staying power over time. This makes sense, doesn't it? You are the most important person in your teen's life, and your teen's anxiety naturally affects, and is affected by, family life.

In this book, I aim to give you all of the tools you need to become an effective anxiety coach for your teen. Before we can start to help teens, though, first we need to learn what really works to reduce anxiety. Did you know that *a huge part of persistent anxiety is a learned response*? This means there are behavioral principles at work that maintain the anxiety over time, and through experience these can be modified. You will learn how to change the factors that keep anxiety at play, including learning to apply the strategies that work best and avoiding those that will inadvertently backfire.

This book also focuses on how your teen's anxiety may have changed how *you* feel and act, too. While you are not to blame for your teen's anxiety, the way you respond to anxious behavior has an important influence. To help decrease your teen's anxiety, you may have pursued some preventive strategies that led to protectiveness, or you may have occasionally given in to demanding requests. Anxious behavior often forces parents to change both normal routines and typical parenting strategies, because anxiety has taken over. It is as if you are now *living by anxiety's rules*, not your own! This book serves as a guide to help free both your teen and you from anxiety's grasp.

Change Is Possible—and Necessary

Don't worry if your teen's anxiety has been around for a while; it is not too late to help. Even teens suffering with anxiety for quite some time can turn a corner. If the anxiety is particularly entrenched, however, your teen might need more time to practice the skills described in this book. Even those who have experienced anxiety for some time have found the techniques to be powerful enough to create immediate positive change in their lives.

This doesn't mean you should underestimate anxiety's negative impact. Some anxiety may subside over the course of your teen's development; however, anxiety that has a significant effect on your teen's everyday functioning rarely goes away on its own. It can worsen over time and potentially have serious consequences. Even if your teen's anxiety is quite mild, teaching him the skills gained from this book will go a long way toward helping him live a more confident and comfortable life. You are, in essence, giving your teen the tools to learn how to better confront scary or stressful situations, which will help your teen deal with any future challenge.

The Basis for This Book

The strategies in this book are based on the cognitive behavioral formulation of anxiety disorders. Cognitive behavioral therapy (CBT), as classically pioneered by Aaron T. Beck, suggests that negative and distressing emotions are caused by certain thoughts, beliefs, and behaviors, which we need to examine and modify in order to reduce those emotions. While that may seem like a simple premise, this therapy carefully prescribes how to properly implement change in a way that has significant, positive, and long-lasting effects on mood and behavior. Ample research suggests that this approach is a safe and effective treatment for anxiety disorders in children and adolescents as well as adults.

The book particularly relies on an ever-growing body of research that suggests that facing your fears through a CBT technique called *exposure with response prevention* is an incredibly effective way to decrease both anxiety and fear-based avoidance. Lastly, the book uses my clinical insights—developed from working with anxious children, adolescents, and their families—into how parents can effectively partner with their children to conquer anxiety. These families, who worked very hard to overcome obstacles to change, have inspired me to share this knowledge.

Who Can This Book Help?

Anxiety can range from mild, infrequent fear all the way up to very debilitating distress. It is important to know that no matter how severe the anxiety, it can respond well to the same core principles that are discussed in this book. This means that your teen does not have to be suffering from an anxiety disorder to benefit from this approach. In fact, I wrote this book to help teens with all levels of anxiety benefit from the fundamental principles. We are also learning that the different types of anxiety problems *share core features, such as behavioral avoidance*, which are addressed in this book.

While this book is aimed at helping teens between the ages of thirteen and nineteen, and considers teen development in applying the techniques, the principles in this book apply to both young and old. Parents of preteens, ages nine to twelve, will find this book relevant and useful. Tweens experience many of the same stressors as older teens and typically respond similarly. If you have a younger child, you will need to be more hands-on in helping her apply the principles. You can also more liberally use rewards to help younger children learn behaviors recommended in this book. Considering their developmental needs, teens will need a lighter touch when parents intervene to help support them.

If you think your teen might be suffering from an anxiety disorder, there is benefit in reaching out for professional help. While this book may be all that a teen with anxiety needs to get a jumpstart on beating his or her fears, it is not a substitute for evaluation or treatment. Teens with certain types of anxiety disorders can especially benefit from clinical guidance. For example, obsessive-compulsive disorder (OCD) responds very well to treatment with a carefully designed CBT treatment program, based on the individual's unique obsessions and compulsions. Use the knowledge gained here to understand how your teen's anxiety works and how you can help, whether or not your teen is in treatment. Your expertise will make a big difference.

How to Use This Book

Chapters 1 and 2 set the foundation for what you need to learn about teen anxiety before you begin trying to effect change. Chapter 1 describes how adolescence primes a teen for anxiety and discusses the varied triggers of anxiety, from biological to cognitive to environmental. Following this, Chapter 2, "The Nuts and Bolts of Parenting An Anxious Teen," explains the basics: which strategies really help anxiety and which ones invariably backfire. With this foundation, you are ready to apply these strategies to dealing with specific problems.

Chapters 3 through 7 delve into five common and distinct ways that anxiety manifests in teens: through constant worry, excessive avoidance, social fearfulness, perfectionism, and irritability. In some cases, these problems can even evolve into enduring patterns of coping behavior, which I would call an *anxious style*. If your teen has developed an entrenched way of responding to anxiety, such as being a worrier, it is especially important to modify it so it does not persist into adulthood.

The focus here is not on diagnosis and treatment of anxiety disorders. Indeed, all anxious teens, no matter the degree of anxiety, can veer into negative patterns of thinking and behavior when they become anxious. In fact, cutting-edge research and treatment for anxiety is beginning to suggest there are fundamental factors found consistently across the range of anxiety disorders, and fundamental treatments that target those factors. This book adopts the same approach.

If your teen is a worrier, pay particular attention to Chapter 3, which describes how to combat worrying and negative thinking. Chapter 4, which discusses what to do when your teen persistently avoids challenging situations, is important to review, because avoidance as a coping mechanism can span multiple types of anxiety. Chapter 5 addresses social fears; Chapter 6 explores perfectionism. If your teen is frequently irritable and overly reactive to stress, you'll benefit particularly from Chapter 7. Each chapter begins with a story that illustrates the particular problem, followed by strategies you can use to manage the problem and teach your teen new skills.

It is best to read the chapters consecutively; this will enrich your understanding of anxiety and broaden your knowledge of key strategies to use. In addition, learning about one anxiety problem will often help you understand another. For example, if your teen is socially fearful, you can benefit from reading about perfectionism, since socially fearful teens can often be quite perfectionistic. If your teen worries a lot, he might avoid many situations that bother him, so reading about behavioral avoidance would be useful. The more you learn about the ways that these problems emerge and interact with one another, the more you can help your teen.

Many teens become fearful of the way anxiety causes physical changes in the body; Chapter 8 explains how to address this problem, with skills for calming both body and mind. Chapter 9 introduces what I call *anxiety flashpoints*—times in your teen's life when she may be particularly vulnerable to anxiety, such as a change of school—and provides some quick tips for managing those situations. Pediatricians provide advice on early childhood development so that you as a parent can monitor for problems and manage them should they arise; this chapter seeks to do the same when it comes to anxiety. The chapter also discusses how to spot and address an anxiety disorder. Chapter 10 focuses on the emotional journey that parents take in supporting their anxious teens, and how to make this journey better, for both yourself and your teen. It provides an eight-point plan for both of you to move in the direction of health and resilience and away from distress.

Each chapter gives you a few activities to try out an important concept. The activities are short and can be completed in a few minutes. Some activities involve brief checklists to complete; a few require that you keep a journal to jot down your ideas. All of the activities are particularly important to review if you would like to serve as a supportive anxiety coach for your teen. The more you use the activities to learn a skill, apply a concept, or better understand your teen, the more the book will come alive for you, and the more effective your actions will be.

A Word About Goal-Setting

I have great confidence that you can use this book to make a significant difference in your teen's life and in her efforts to overcome anxiety. However, as you read this book, be sure to set realistic goals. Anxiety is a normal, adaptive human response. We don't want to completely eliminate it. Let's identify the ways that anxiety is causing *too much* distress or dysfunction in your teen's life and then work to reduce it. While you can't do the hard work of eliminating anxiety for your teen, your guidance, praise, and direction will go a long way toward helping conquer your teen's fears. Don't be discouraged if change takes time. *And remember: every little change counts.*

1 Teens and Anxiety: A Perfect Storm

Understanding Anxiety and the Unique Nature of Adolescent Fears

"Michael is always worried about something, even the smallest thing. He frequently needs reassurance, but he never seems to feel better for long. Sometimes he thinks that everything has gone wrong. I just wish that he could relax more."

"Madeline is our high-achiever. She really tries hard and can't stop working until her projects are perfect. No matter the grade, she never thinks her work is good enough. Lately she has been really tearful about school. I think the stress is getting to her."

"Olivia is worried about behaving foolishly. I wish that she would not be so focused on what everyone else thinks of her. It has gotten to the point where she avoids calling any attention to herself. I was heartbroken when she wouldn't try out for the musical even though she really wanted to."

"Amy is now just flat out refusing to do many things when she is afraid. She got upset about going to the soccer game and then wouldn't go. On the day of her test, she complained of feeling unwell and missed it. How do I break this pattern?"

"John has been taking his stress out on the whole family. He overreacts to little things and snaps at his younger brother. He even had a major meltdown the other day. Sometimes we are at our wits' end as to what to do."

Anxiety's Far-Reaching Impact

The teens you have just heard about all suffer from the different ways in which anxiety manifests, each with its own unique hardships. Anxiety is a pervasive and growing problem in America today. Current estimates suggest that about one in five adolescents in America suffers from a clinical anxiety disorder. These are in fact the most common psychiatric disorders of childhood. Countless other teens struggle with daily stress and worry that have profound effects on their lives.

The Consequences of Teen Anxiety

Nobody knows more than you the toll that anxiety can take on your teen. It can interfere with your teen's academics, family life, peer relations, and overall emotional state. Teens who are anxious are often less able to concentrate in school, so their schoolwork and grades may suffer. Anxious teens can become irritable and overwhelmed or, in the worst cases, experience all-out panic attacks. Those with social anxiety avoid taking social risks and thus become more socially isolated. Anxiety can even be at the root of substance abuse, when teens self-medicate to try to reduce their uncomfortable feelings.

The longer-term effects of having anxiety become even more significant. In their effort to preserve a sense of safety, anxious teens often avoid trying out new challenges and taking reasonable risks in life. This pattern of avoidance can seriously impact identity, confidence, and skills development over time. Severe avoidance can even take teens off a normal developmental path to the point that they fall behind their peers in important areas of their lives.

Once anxiety develops into a full-blown anxiety disorder, a teen also is at risk for developing other psychiatric disorders, particularly depression. Worst of all, unless teen anxiety is managed, teens are at risk for developing a chronic anxiety disorder, which can persist into adulthood and have far-reaching effects on relationships, jobs, and quality of life.

The Many Faces of Anxiety in Teens

Anxiety in teens shows up in different ways. Many teens worry and brood about their problems. Perhaps you notice that your son or daughter seems to worry about every little thing, and minor setbacks are blown up into something incredibly major. Teen worriers contemplate lots of "What if" questions about the future and find it difficult to tolerate uncertain situations. They also express anxiety through fearful behavior. Anxious teens stay vigilant to recognize threats in the outside world, and they avoid situations they consider potentially dangerous.

The way teens perceive themselves and imagine how others perceive them is often fraught with anxiety. Social anxiety, in particular, can emerge during adolescence, as teens are constantly on the lookout to avoid embarrassment. Perfectionism also plagues many teens: no matter how hard they try, nothing they do seems good enough. Frequently, teens may express anxiety through irritable mood and behavior.

Despite these variations in how anxiety is exhibited, most people with anxiety have two things in common—an exaggerated sense that the world is a dangerous place, and ongoing attempts to cope in ways that minimize this danger.

Where Does Anxiety Come From?

We have all experienced anxiety at one time or another, yet we may not stop to think about where it comes from. It seems an awful lot like fear; this is true in that both involve a feeling that we are in danger. Yet fear is an *immediate reaction to a real threat* and is a biologically driven survival response, like when we reflexively pull back if we touch something hot. For example, if we jump out of the way of a car careening toward us, we are not spending a lot of time thinking; we are just acting adaptively in the moment, and a burst of fear helps us to do that. Anxiety is much more complex. Indeed, anxiety's true nature is like a quilt, patched together from multiple and varied sources.

The Biological Origins of Anxiety

Anxiety is our internal alarm system notifying us that danger is close at hand and we must be ready for it. It is healthy and necessary because we all need this adaptive response to danger. Otherwise, we would be less vigilant about our surroundings. Scientists believe that we developed this internal sensor for danger through an evolutionary process. In other words, anxiety developed to help us survive.

You may have heard of a physiological mechanism that arose from our evolutionary past: the fight-or-flight response. When this response is triggered by a situation we feel threatens our survival, a cascade of chemicals initiates changes in our body, preparing us to either fight or flee. This change in our physical state can have unpleasant side effects: stomachaches, dizziness, sweating, and other uncomfortable sensations. The problem is, today we are no longer facing beasts in the jungle, yet *our internal alarm system is still easily triggered*. For example, most of us can remember having to give a presentation in class and noticing our heart starting to race and our palms getting sweaty. Although we were not really in danger, our body had gone into full alert mode.

Some people are genetically predisposed to be more anxious. This means anxiety disorders can run in a family. Remarkably, if a parent suffers from a diagnosed anxiety disorder, a child is up to seven times more likely than a child whose parent does not have an anxiety disorder to suffer from one as well. Children do not directly inherit a specific anxiety disorder from their parents; rather, they may inherit a predisposition to be sensitive and fearful and to experience more frequent negative emotions. Children who inherit this vulnerability rarely outgrow it. So, over time, a full-blown anxiety disorder may develop.

The Cognitive Triggers of Anxiety

At its most basic, anxiety is a fear or nervousness about what might happen in the future, particularly about whether something threatening or dangerous will occur. This nervous apprehension is therefore a cognitive process and can be triggered by our specific perceptions of situations. Keep in mind that what is classified as dangerous varies from person to person and can be highly subjective. Some perceptions of danger are based on real-life dangers, such as fear of being in a plane crash, whereas others are more abstract and highly subjective, such as social fears. Our anxious mind, even if it gets the best of us, is the aspect of anxiety over which we have the greatest control. We'll return to this later.

The Behavioral Triggers of Anxiety

It is natural to assume that anxious behavior is a part of anxiety itself, which of course is true. However, *anxious behavior actually causes anxiety* as well. This occurs when people attempt to cope by repeatedly avoiding what they fear. Avoidance of a feared situation reduces anxiety; however, it then triggers even more anxiety over time. By not confronting their fears, people never learn that what they fear is not as bad as they thought. Therefore, anxiety is caused in part by a learning process—I learn that avoiding makes me feel better for now, but I don't learn that facing unrealistic fears is not as dangerous or intolerable as I fear it is.

The Physiological Triggers of Anxiety

Along with our thoughts and behaviors, the physical signs of anxiety are both a component of the anxiety and, often, a trigger for further anxiety. When we experience sudden fear, we can experience a stomachache, a rapid heart rate, shortness of breath, and other uncomfortable body sensations. These symptoms, again, are biologically linked to the fight-or-flight response. Anxiety can trigger those same sensations and prolong them through the way we interpret our physical symptoms.

People often misinterpret the physical component of anxiety as a physical illness. It then serves as a trigger for more anxiety. For example, a teen might worry that she is ill when she just has an upset stomach because she is anxious. If these physical changes are severe enough—for example, feeling that we can't breathe—we may conclude that we are in significant danger, thus setting off more anxiety.

The Perpetual Anxiety Cycle

Each of the multiple cognitive, physiological, and behavioral influences on anxiety can make anxiety worse on its own. Yet, even more important, a vicious cycle develops in which *all the triggers of anxiety interact* to heighten the discomfort. For example, anxious thoughts trigger anxious feelings and uncomfortable body sensations, which increase behavioral avoidance. Behavioral avoidance then triggers more anxious thoughts, since we are not confronting our fears (see Figure 1.1).

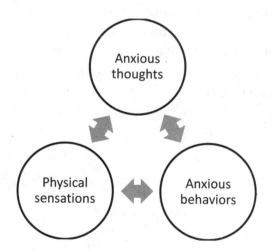

Figure 1.1. A Vicious Cycle: Thoughts, Physical Sensations, and Behaviors Interact to Worsen Anxiety

Here is an example of the way thoughts, feelings, and behaviors interact to heighten anxiety in a seventeen-year-old experiencing her first panic attack:

- **Physical symptom**: Suddenly feeling light-headed and breathing rapidly.

- **Thought**: *I can't breathe. I might faint and fall down in front of everyone.*

- **Feeling**: Highly anxious.

- **Behavior**: Avoiding situations where she experiences feelings of panic.

- **Next Thought**: *As long as I avoid certain places, I am safe. Otherwise, something really bad and embarrassing will happen to me.*

- **Next Physical Symptom**: Heightened dizziness and physical distress when entering a "dangerous" situation.

- **Next Feeling**: Relief after each instance of avoidance. Even more heightened anxiety and panic when she enters the scary situation.

- **Next Behavior**: Continued and increased avoidance.

Activity: My Teen's Anxiety Cycle

Try thinking about the ways in which your teen's anxious thoughts, feelings, and behaviors contribute to his anxiety cycle. What thoughts tend to trigger anxious feelings? What behaviors does your teen engage in to cope with those feelings? Do those behaviors trigger new thoughts and new behaviors? Write down what you have discovered. Doing this exercise will help you identify the distinct components of your teen's anxiety and allow you to see how these components might interact with each other. Save this information for later when you help your teen change his anxious thoughts and behaviors.

Why Are Teens Prone to Anxiety?

During this crucial life stage, what could be happening to make your teen so anxious? The teen years are a heady mix of brain development, hormonal changes, identity formulation, and increased stress. As you learn more about these factors, keep them in mind when you try to help your teen; this will increase your awareness of what triggers her anxiety.

Your Teen's Brain Is Reinventing Itself

Did you know that the brain undergoes remarkable changes during adolescence, beginning a remodeling process that continues through early adulthood? Beginning around age twelve and continuing through adolescence, there is a growth spurt in the frontal cortex, the area of the brain responsible for logic and judgment. During adolescence there is also a period of reorganization, which involves shedding of certain neural connections, strengthening of other connections, and continuing growth and change in brain structure. This brain change has an impact on adolescent behavior, both positive and negative.

On the positive side, as the frontal cortex and brain connections become more developed, adolescents demonstrate an improved ability to learn and engage in abstract reasoning. Now they can grapple with deeper issues, such as developing their identity and forming life goals. This is also why your son or daughter is now such a good debater and loves to question your point of view. Compared to adults, teens are like sponges, picking up information at a faster pace during these years.

However, despite the positive growth in brain development, *the adolescent brain does not fully mature until the mid-twenties.* Moreover, the areas responsible for planning and impulse control are the last to mature. What all of this means for adolescents is that gaining the cognitive skills that affect control over emotions—such as planning, impulse control, and judgment—is still a work in progress. Therefore, a teen's emotions can still easily interfere with logic. In fact, much adolescent moodiness, which was previously attributed to hormonal shifts, is now recognized as a consequence of the developing brain. In addition, the cognitive changes in the teen brain that improve abstract thinking unfortunately also allow teens to better anticipate the possibility of negative events happening. What does all of this produce for your teen? Lots of anxiety and doubt.

Your Teen's Body Is Changing

While this brain change is happening, other important biological changes are occurring. *The period of adolescence is defined by the onset of puberty.* During puberty there are changes in hormones that, added to brain changes, can intensify feelings. The body changes of puberty often bring on discomfort and insecurity. And biological changes in adolescent sleep patterns make it harder for your teen both to go to sleep and to wake up, which also affects mood.

Critically, certain genes that children inherit from their parents are often activated during puberty. So if you or a relative have inherited some degree of a propensity for anxiety, your child in turn may begin to show signs of this biologically driven vulnerability during puberty. Some anxiety disorders are typically diagnosed during adolescence, in part for this reason.

Your Teen's Identity Is Developing

Figuring out identity is a key task of adolescence, and how they fit in socially is a predominant identity concern for teens. This is true for all adolescents, whether they experience significant anxiety or not. In adolescence, teens feel their standing in the world is now judged by what type of friends they have and how many. So now teens worry about how they appear to others and wonder if they are popular or cool enough.

Under this pressure, teens prone to anxiety become particularly attuned to social threats, always surveying the social landscape to avoid accidentally stepping on a landmine. They constantly check to see if they are saying the right thing and wearing the right thing. This level of personal self-scrutiny increases both social anxiety and anxiety in general. Not surprisingly, then, *one of the most common anxiety disorders of adolescence is social anxiety disorder.*

Teens forming their identity can also begin to develop performance fears. Many worry about whether they will achieve their goals, and some, as they approach adulthood, have a flawed belief that they must perform perfectly in everything they do. This places tremendous pressure on teens who may need extra time to figure out their identity, expand their skills, or simply mature.

Your Teen Faces High Stress and Higher Expectations

Now that teens are in the midst of huge cognitive, social, and biological changes, can we give them a break and make life a little easier for a while? Nope! Stress rears its ugly head. There are numerous new pressures to confront, causing teens to quickly become overwhelmed.

Academic demands are the most common trigger of stress during this time. Many adolescents worry about making good grades, think "average" grades are inferior, and view tests as a serious measure of their worth. Teens also experience frequent time pressure that they won't get everything done. These feelings are in part anxiety talking and in part based on the real burden of extra homework and a busier lifestyle for this generation of teens.

Along with a higher level of stress, teens suddenly face higher expectations from others. Parents, teachers, coaches, and colleges all expect a lot from this generation. Teens are asked to not only quickly juggle multiple responsibilities but also perform well in all of them. Unfortunately, these demands sometimes exceed their capacity for coping.

Teens internalize these high expectations and now place the same pressure—or more—on themselves to perform well. They worry about keeping up with their peers and whether their parents will be disappointed with their performance. Some think that everything—*their whole life!*—rides on how they do now. And they haven't even fully developed confidence in their ability to face life's challenges. This is a recipe for burgeoning anxiety.

Stumbling Blocks to Helping Your Anxious Teen

In this chapter we've considered the origins of teen anxiety from a developmental standpoint. Before we move on to what we can do about anxiety, we have to consider the impact of teen development on the relationship between parents and anxious teens. Here are a few stumbling blocks that may appear when you try to help your anxious teen.

Your Teen Lets You in Less Often

Many a parent has wondered, "Why does my teen suddenly not want to talk to me anymore? We used to talk all the time. Now he just stays in his room." This behavior demonstrates a push for independence, which is a normal part of adolescence. However, it makes it very hard to know what is going on with your teen. When you ask how things are going, your teen often just says "Fine." It's now harder to find out what is happening inside their minds, including whether they are feeling anxious. You watch for signs of trouble, but…

Your Teen's Anxiety Goes Undercover

Many teens suffer in silence. They exhibit an outward façade of calm that belies the tension they feel. They put on a good show until, with high enough stress and inadequate coping, their anxiety comes bursting out. This building of hidden tension and worry without enough outlets for relief often makes anxiety significantly worse. It can make it especially tough for parents to intervene early on to prevent their teen's anxiety from worsening. When your teen exhibits signs of distress, you try to step in, but…

Your Teen Resists Your Input

Often, when you try to help your teen solve her worries, you get serious pushback. Your teen, wanting to be more independent, sometimes prefers to handle problems her way. In fact, with her newly enhanced reasoning abilities, she will question everything, including your advice. In many cases, teens feel parents don't understand what they are going through. That may often be true, since their anxiety is highly subjective and parents know less about what is going on in their teens' lives than they did when their teens were small children. So when you suggest that your young teen sit in the cafeteria with a friend she hasn't hung out with in two years, she looks at you with horror— how could you be so clueless! You try to encourage her to face her fears, but…

Your Teen Easily Avoids Confronting Challenges

When our kids were toddlers facing the first day of preschool, if they didn't want to go, we could just pick them up and take them to face and overcome their fear. Our kids are a lot heavier now!

Teens are pretty masterful at avoiding challenges they don't want to confront, and often their avoidance flies under the radar. They may not try out for a play for fear of doing something embarrassing, and sometimes we don't even realize the tryout has already come and gone. They avoid studying for a test due to anxiety, and we may mistake this for laziness. Even if you are aware of your teen's avoidance, it is very challenging to get him to stop. You can't force him to go places or do things. During the teen years, avoidance is particularly difficult to overcome.

What's Next?

Now we can clearly see the burden that many teens with anxiety face and why we sometimes have difficulty intervening to support them. But don't be disheartened. You'll soon learn some excellent ways to step in with anxious teens, ways that take into account the challenges they face and the common communication barriers. Your teen also has individual strengths to rely on that he can harness with your support.

As you read further, keep in mind this information about teen development and the factors that affect teen stress and anxiety. This will put into context the fears that your teen expresses and help you consider sensitive ways to intervene. In the next chapter you will get a broad overview of which strategies are especially helpful when dealing with an anxious teen. Although the teen years are a ripe time for anxiety, they can also be a ripe time for action. Let's begin creating positive change.

2 The Nuts and Bolts of Parenting an Anxious Teen

What Works and What Backfires When Managing Teen Anxiety

This chapter is designed to help you begin to differentiate between strategies that genuinely keep anxiety at bay and strategies that tend to not work well or even backfire, making anxiety worse. Cutting-edge research and treatments for anxiety are now suggesting that despite the variance in how anxiety manifests from one problem to the next, all types of maladaptive anxiety share certain core features that maintain the problem. By targeting those features, we can best alleviate the anxiety. Therefore, learning broadly effective principles for managing anxiety will help you develop a good foundation for reducing anxiety, regardless of the specific type of anxiety your teen exhibits.

Strategies That Don't Work Well to Reduce Anxiety

Most parents at one time or another have used strategies that don't seem to diminish their teen's anxiety very much. In fact, you may be reading this book to discover a new, more effective approach to dealing with those fears. Your teen has probably also tried some coping strategies that turned out to be ineffective. Neither you nor your teen are to blame for the anxiety that continues to be so troublesome. As discussed in Chapter 1, anxiety arises from multiple sources. In addition, some strategies actually work in the short term but don't have the intended effect of reducing anxiety in the long run. It is time to view anxiety as a trap that has drawn both you and your teen into behaviors that ended up worsening anxiety.

Here are some commonly used strategies that *don't* work well to reduce anxiety.

Telling Your Teen to Stop Thinking About It

This is a common and natural reaction to anxiety's incessant drumbeat. Your teen might tell you his worries, perhaps when things feel really bad, and you try to encourage him to let go of his fears. But the worries won't budge, and he keeps expressing them, over and over. You want your teen to feel better, or perhaps you feel a little exasperated with his repetitive complaints, so in the end you say, *"Just stop thinking about it."*

The problem with this approach is that we can't just suppress our fears. Fears are not so easily dismissed. In fact, this advice may have the opposite effect. In an interesting study by Harvard psychologist Daniel Wegner, people were asked to not think of a white bear and then later told to deliberately hold the thought of a white bear in their mind. He and his colleagues found that when subjects tried to suppress thoughts of the white bear, the suppression immediately increased those thoughts rather than decreasing them.

More recent research has corroborated that thought suppression really doesn't work. When a teen attempts to block the thoughts that cause anxiety, it can make those fearful thoughts more frequent and noticeable. Successful strategies for getting thoughts "unstuck" are often counterintuitive. By trying to think of something else, you think of it more, but by trying to think of it more, you often end up thinking of it less! I often guide kids and teens whom I work with through a fun exercise, "Think About Red Sheep," to help them recognize this phenomenon. Try it out for yourself.

Activity: Think About Red Sheep

Imagine a red sheep among many white sheep. Notice the vivid color of the red against the backdrop of fluffy white sheep. What particular color red is the sheep? Now that you have a vivid mental image, try something new. When I say "Begin," try your best for five minutes to avoid thinking about red sheep. Just do your best to avoid thinking about the red sheep. Push it out of your mind. Now begin…

What did you notice? I bet you noticed that no matter how hard you tried to not think about the red sheep, you couldn't help having it pop up in your mind!

Now try another experiment. Do your best to keep thinking about the red sheep. Recite it over and over and never let it leave your mind. Keep going for as long as you can…*red sheep, red sheep, red sheep, red sheep, red sheep, red sheep*…keep going.

What did you observe? Did you start to think about being hungry or something you forgot to do? Notice that the more we try to hold a thought in our mind, the harder it is to hang onto it. Sooner or later our thoughts will focus on something else.

Jumping in with Advice

Most parents naturally impart their wisdom to a teen facing any kind of challenge, but when it comes to anxiety, advice rarely works well. Why is that? There are many reasons. First, often you give advice when your teen is at the height of his anxiety, but during those times he is unable to even process the advice. Since parents often offer this advice without first fully empathizing with their teen, it can also unintentionally make teens feel that their feelings are not important. This happens particularly if a parent demands that the teen quickly make a change, which the teen might be unprepared to do. A second problem is that in giving advice parents rarely consider that fears are highly subjective. Although parents naturally want to minimize the teen's perception of a threat as quickly as possible, sometimes the advice misses its mark completely by ignoring the unique way the teen is perceiving a situation. For example, test anxiety might be due to fear of imperfection, fear of disappointing a teacher, fear of social disapproval from peers, fear of running out of time—the list goes on. Parents have to engage with their teens to first understand *why* a situation feels so dangerous. Only then can they help combat anxiety from their teen's perspective.

On top of those problems, teens, being at the stage of development in which they value independence, often resist advice. The more a parent tries to assert control and talk the teen out of being anxious, the more the teen may avoid responding. Finally, and most important, advice-giving tells a teen *what to think and do* but does not teach a teen *how to think and behave* when anxious. As will be discussed later in the chapter, teens do best when they learn a systematic way of thinking and acting in response to anxiety, no matter the specific fear. Parents can help with this new learning, but they can't always lead the way.

Allowing Avoidance of Fears

When anxiety hits, almost all parents begin to adapt and modify their own behaviors to reduce their teen's anxiety. We most often do this by helping a teen to avoid threatening situations. For example, a parent might speak to a coach on behalf of her socially anxious teen, or turn the door handle for a teen afraid of germs. It is hard for parents to resist this push for avoidance, because teens can be very insistent when distressed, and the avoidance gives some relief, even if temporary. Gradually, though, parents modify more and more of their behaviors and family routines in an effort to help their teen avoid feeling anxious.

Allowing avoidance, even if it removes anxiety temporarily, has a big downside. In the short term, it reduces your teen's ability to cope with the triggers of her anxiety and with her own anxious feelings. For example, if a parent allows a teen with test anxiety to stay at home on the day of a test, that teen doesn't learn how to cope with test-taking the next time around or to successfully handle feeling nervous.

In the long term, *the more avoidance takes hold, the more anxiety becomes stuck,* because by avoiding, teens don't get to learn that the situations they avoid are *not* dangerous or intolerable. The other problem is that any behavior that is rewarded will naturally occur more often. Avoidance as a behavior tends to get rewarded because avoiding something fearful brings such great relief. Teens who avoid may also inadvertently experience secondary rewards, such as attention or a removal of other stressors in their environment. Ultimately, avoidance is an ineffective coping strategy that keeps anxiety going.

Activity: How Does My Teen Push to Avoid?

Consider whether there are ways that your teen is pushing you to change your behavior (to do things or not do things) so she can avoid feeling anxious. Does she ask you to do things for her to help her avoid? Does she push to have a change in household rules to help her to avoid? Does she push you to stay with her to help her avoid? Write down what you notice, and save this information for later. In Chapter 4 you will learn how to systematically decrease your teen's avoidance.

Giving Excessive Reassurance

One of the most natural things for all parents to do is to reassure their children that everything is all right and that they are safe. If you have a teen experiencing chronic anxiety, you may have been repeatedly asked in one form or another, "Will I be okay?" Your teen may rely on such reassurance to relieve his anxiety. Yet those of us who treat anxious kids see that excessive reassurance doesn't actually help with persistent anxiety. In fact, it can make it worse!

How can that be? Think of anxiety as a chain reaction, which includes the trigger (what made us anxious) and then the response (what we do when we are anxious). When our anxiety is triggered, our anxiety shoots up, and we look for ways to bring it down. Reassurance quickly brings the anxiety down, which serves to reinforce the behavior of seeking reassurance and makes us turn to it the next time around. And the removal of distress serves as a form of avoidance, which, as was just mentioned, strengthens fears. Through this type of avoidance, teens never learn that they can tolerate the anxiety that the reassurance was taking away.

Parents soon realize that repeated reassurance never really works to eliminate anxiety for long—it just pops back up when the next anxiety trigger occurs. On top of that, instead of decreasing over time, the need for reassurance often steadily increases. It becomes clear the quick fix makes the problem worse in the long run!

You may be wondering, "What if my teen really is misperceiving how dangerous a situation is through a simple lack of knowing the facts?" A small amount of reassurance is okay, especially if it corrects misinformation that a teen has about something. For example, a teen who experiences rapid heartbeat and dizziness due to having a panic attack needs reassurance that her physical symptoms are not dangerous and are just a sign of acute anxiety. Once your teen has received education and reassurance to correct misunderstandings and misperceptions, it's time to avoid responding to repetitive questions of the same nature. As well, if you respond to a seemingly new "What if" question every day, let your teen know that you both need to avoid strengthening fears by playing the reassurance game. Before making this change, give your teen a heads-up that you will be gradually reducing reassurance, and express confidence in her ability to get through her feelings of uncertainty.

Activity: What Isn't Working?

Now that you understand some common strategies that typically *don't* work to reduce anxiety, think back to what you have tried. What did you notice?

☐   I told my teen to stop thinking about it.

☐   I jumped in too quickly with advice.

☐   I got caught by the avoidance trap.

☐   I fell into the reassurance trap.

Now ask yourself the following questions:

- What was the outcome of the strategy or strategies that I checked off in the first list?

- Did my strategy work? If so, how well and how often did it work?

- Did my strategy help a little but only in the short term or not enough?

- Did it not work at all or backfire, making my teen's anxiety worse?

Thinking carefully about the results of your approach will help you decide which strategies to consider changing. A downloadable worksheet is available at http://www.newharbinger.com/34657. (See the back of the book for more information.)

Parenting Strategies That Really Work!

Despite the pitfalls that parents can encounter when they try to help anxious teens, it is never too late to learn and implement strategies that truly get through to your teen and make a difference. The strategies described next all build on each other and are designed to work together for the best results. Later, these strategies will be applied to addressing specific problems and become a routine part of your tool kit for helping your anxious teen.

Connect Before You Correct

Even if parents express confidence in their teen's ability to face fearful challenges, if teens feel that parents don't understand what they are going through, they usually resist the advice. For example, if a parent starts by saying, "Don't be afraid. It's not that bad," it can unwittingly make a teen feel like the parent just doesn't get it! To help teens, we have to first bridge the gap in communication and connect with them.

There are two key ways you can build connection with your teen when he is in the midst of an anxious moment: empathy and active listening. To empathize means to put yourself in the teen's shoes to understand what he might be feeling. To engage in active listening means to reflect back what you hear him saying, to make sure your understanding is correct. The goal at this point is not to try to change your teen's perspective on his situation, but to show that you truly understand what he is thinking and feeling.

The following is an example of a parent conveying both empathy and active listening to demonstrate that a worry is understood:

Teen: I tried to fix the project, but now it's ruined! What if the teacher gives me a terrible grade? I need at least a B for the marking period or else my GPA is going to stink!

Parent: You seem really worried that you made a big mistake that might hurt your GPA. That must feel incredibly concerning to you.

You should engage in empathy and active listening even if you believe that the fears are exaggerated or completely unfounded or that your teen's behavior is giving in to the fear. Through feeling empathized with and understood, your teen will be more willing to let you in and allow you to help him.

Externalize the Anxiety and Talk Back to It

A great way to reduce anxiety's power is to first externalize it as something separate from yourself and then talk back to it, telling anxiety that you won't listen to its tricks. That simple strategy serves as a one-two punch, helping to make anxiety easier to challenge and overcome. For example, instead of teens thinking *I can't handle things right now*, they can say to themselves, *Anxiety has made me think that this is too tough to deal with, but I don't have to listen to its tricks.*

Sometimes it helps to give anxiety a personalized nickname (along with an image, if that appeals). Often younger kids enjoy personalized nicknames more than older ones, but let your teen decide what works for her. Your teen can pick out what she would like to call her anxiety. Besides calling it the obvious—anxiety!—some other possibilities are "fears," "worries," "stuck thoughts," "spam," or anything else she wishes. I often recommend initials or acronyms for teens to try. One teen thought of calling her anxiety "OTT" for "over-the-top fears"!

Once your teen decides what to call his anxiety, encourage him to begin talking back to it in his mind whenever he is anxious, with the goal of listening to it less and focusing more on what he wants to do in the moment. If your teen gets really stuck, with his permission you can help him talk back to the anxiety as well. Anxiety usually also makes us focus on things that are not really important in our lives. Talking back to anxiety is designed to call it out for what it really is—a *false alarm*.

Team Up with Your Teen

Anxiety often pits teens and parents against each other in ways that neither of you wants. This typically occurs when teens avoid something important that their parents want them to face. For example, they might threaten to avoid a social, academic, or sports activity that their parents would like them to attend. Parents in this situation often argue with their teen about this behavior and insist on a change. But we can't just demand that anxiety leave. With that approach, more often than not, teens stubbornly refuse to give in, and they maintain their avoidant behavior.

Teaming up with your teen means helping her see that the two of you are on the same side against anxiety. Make anxiety the opponent by identifying it, not your teen's behavior, as the problem. Then encourage her to partner with you to defeat it. The advantage to parents and teens in using this strategy is that it also helps to take the blame off the teen for her anxious behavior. Then she will be more receptive to taking your advice when you give it.

Again, parents can effectively make anxiety the opponent, just as their teen can, by externalizing the anxiety and talking back to it with their teen. For example, here's an *ineffective* way for a parent to respond: "You can't just miss the event because you are upset. Stop being so stubborn, and come with us." A more effective approach would be "I see that anxiety has gotten you stuck. Let's see how we can work together to stop anxiety from making you miss the event." Now, rather than the teen being blamed, anxiety becomes the opponent that together you work on and defeat.

Help Your Teen Challenge Negative Thinking

A key premise of this book, and of the cognitive behavioral theory of anxiety, is that anxiety is caused in large part by the specific and faulty ways that we perceive events. Teens with anxiety tend to view situations as more dangerous than they really are. This occurs because anxious thoughts tend to contain "thinking errors"—negative thinking patterns that can trigger anxiety because they are unrealistic. The following list of key errors in thinking was developed by Aaron T. Beck, M.D., and popularized by David D. Burns, M.D., both pioneers of cognitive behavioral therapy.

Common Thinking Errors

All-or-Nothing Thinking: Viewing situations in black-and-white extremes, as either good or bad, perfect or a failure.

Mental Filter: Noticing only the negatives.

Disqualifying the Positive: Completely discounting positive events when they occur.

Mind Reading: Jumping to the conclusion that someone perceives you negatively.

Catastrophizing: Fearing the worst.

Overgeneralization: Making a too-broad conclusion based on a single event or single piece of evidence; in particular, viewing a single event as a sign of a continuing pattern of defeat.

All of us at times engage in these errors in thinking; however, overcoming them is not easy, since we tend to not even notice that we are making them. To help your teen feel less anxious, you need to first guide him to notice the thoughts that trigger anxiety, and then help him to evaluate these thoughts. We evaluate thoughts by asking, *What is the evidence for and against the thought?* This squarely puts thoughts to the test as to whether they are faulty. Then, using this information, we encourage more realistic thinking.

Teens often resist well-meaning advice from their parents about how they are not perceiving a situation correctly. So, to get through to your teen, the best way to challenge faulty thinking is through a technique called *Socratic questioning,* based on a form of inquiry pioneered by the Greek philosopher Socrates to stimulate critical thinking. Rather than telling your teen what to think, this technique involves *asking questions* to elicit negative or anxious thoughts. Once the questions uncover your teen's specific worries, they can be used to overcome negative thoughts and even encourage your teen to see that she can cope with a problem. For example, if your teen is expecting the worst outcome possible (an example of catastrophizing), you can say, "Is there a way that the situation may be less bad than it seems?" The following questions can be helpful.

Socratic Questions to Identify and Challenge Anxious Thoughts

- What are your fears saying?

- What worries you?

- Are there some reasons why your worries may not be true?

- Could you be fearing the worst?

- What could happen instead?

- What is another way to look at it?

- Could the situation be less bad than it seems?

- Are there any positives to the situation that you are overlooking?

- If what you fear really happened, could it be less important than you think, or could you somehow deal with it?

A few general principles for Socratic questioning: Make sure not to overdo it—like salt, you can always add a little more emphasis later. Gentle tone of voice is important, as appearing demanding will quickly shut down communication. Give your teen a chance to consider a question or two to view his thoughts from a different perspective. The key is to *gently question, not give advice,* and to allow your teen to identify and then challenge the worry on his own. In future chapters you'll learn to apply this strategy to a variety of concerns, from avoidance to perfectionism, social fears to stress. No matter the content of the worry, this strategy cues your teen to not accept his worries at face value.

Redirect to Problem-Solving

If your teen is struggling with a real-life problem, switch to a calm problem-solving approach, rather than challenging faulty thinking. In this case, guide your teen to find all of the possible solutions to a problem before she decides that a problem is unsolvable. Then ask her to *evaluate the merits of each solution* before she discards it. Finally, encourage your teen to choose a solution and go for it! This problem-solving approach forces your teen to apply logic to a highly emotional situation. It also seems to naturally diminish the severity of the problem in her mind.

For example, one teen became very upset when she left the crucial instructions and partially done work for an assignment in her locker over the weekend. She immediately imagined that she would now fail the project and her life would be ruined! Her parent guided her to brainstorm what to do, which included the following: see if someone will let you into the school, call a friend to go over the instructions, e-mail the teacher for help, ask the teacher for an extension on Monday, or accept a small penalty for lateness. By identifying these different possibilities, even the imperfect ones, she began seeing the problem as one that was both solvable and noncatastrophic.

Attend to Non-Anxious Behavior

There is actually one simple, effective way that you can decrease your teen's anxious behavior that doesn't even require her participation: change *how you respond* to the anxious behavior when it occurs. Anxious behavior typically draws lots of attention, which inadvertently is positively reinforcing. This means that attention rewards anxiety, making anxiety more likely to occur in the future. It is not that your teen is deliberately trying to be rewarded by getting anxious, but the anxious behavior gets reinforced anyway. By paying more attention to non-anxious behavior, you turn the tables on anxiety by rewarding it less. Remember the important rule here: pay more attention to the behavior you are trying to increase rather than attending more often to the behavior you are trying to decrease.

The way to do this in practice is to catch your teen when he is displaying non-anxious behavior, or especially when he is displaying brave behavior, and attend to it; for example:

- Pay more attention to your teen when calm behavior is displayed.

- Acknowledge calm behavior as soon as it occurs.

- Acknowledge brave behavior as soon as it occurs.

- Deliberately ignore anxious behavior when it is occurring.

Using the phrase "I notice that you…" helps to identify what specific behavior you are acknowledging. For example, you can say, "I notice that you really pushed yourself to go to school today even though you didn't want to go." Also keep in mind that reinforcement is most powerful when it is done close in time to a behavior, so don't wait to respond with positive attention. By implementing this strategy consistently over time, you can subtly and powerfully shift how anxiety is responded to and how often it gets rewarded.

Stop Dancing to Anxiety's Tune

Life often grinds to a halt in many households because of anxiety. It seems that parents are always playing defense, trying to prevent anxiety's impact on their child and family. It is important for parents to instead establish an atmosphere where anxiety is not the most important member of the household! This means the rules and routines of the household remain as they were before the anxiety took hold. This goes hand in hand with reducing avoidance. It also means that parents don't work hard to anticipate ways to decrease their teen's anxiety. If a parent is constantly bending to the demands of an anxious teen to protect her from experiencing anxiety, then the teen is not getting enough opportunities to practice positive coping. Tell your teen it is time for both of you to _not play by anxiety's rules anymore_; then gradually, over time, reduce behaviors that protect her from experiencing anxiety.

Research backs up the importance of this approach. In a now landmark study on obsessive-compulsive disorder, the Pediatric Obsessive Compulsive Treatment Study, Abbe Garcia and her colleagues found that the more families modified their behavior and routines in response to OCD, the worse their kids responded to treatment, whether it was CBT, medication, or a combination of both. And in another study by John Piacentini and his fellow researchers, when parents became less involved in protecting their teen from anxiety, this predicted improvement in anxiety symptoms. So when parents give in to anxiety's demands, it worsens the chance for recovery, whereas doing the opposite helps take the anxiety away. This shows the remarkable power of a parent's role in helping a teen overcome anxiety.

In addition to reducing accommodation to anxiety, you can normalize anxiety, which means conveying that it is to be expected; we all experience it at times, and we don't stop what we are doing because of it. Your teen needs to develop a new attitude toward anxiety, to see it as something that comes along for the ride, rather than as a load too heavy to bear.

Encourage Tolerance of Uncertainty and Risk

Sometimes you have to employ counterintuitive strategies to defeat anxiety. As discussed earlier, reassuring away the fear might temporarily help to reduce anxiety, but it doesn't defeat it in the long run. In fact, the thing about worries is that even if there is only a thousandth or a millionth of a chance of something bad happening, a worry can still stick around. Anxious individuals *crave the certainty of complete safety*, which, as we know, is an illusion. Instead of giving in to this illusion, we have to allow our anxious teens to see that risk of harm, though it may be rare, cannot be eliminated. Despite this, we need to encourage teens to keep taking reasonable risks in life in order to grow and become fully developed human beings.

The best approach to teaching this way of being is to frame the most feared outcomes as possible, but highly improbable, and something to accept while going about the business of life. For example, instead of your reflexive response of quickly reassuring, gradually reduce reassurance over time to leave open a little room for doubt about whether danger exists. Then encourage your teen to tolerate any uncertainty he feels while continuing to take necessary action. The most powerful way to help him practice tolerating uncertainty and risk is through a technique called *exposure*, which we will consider shortly.

Encourage Small Steps Toward Change

Many teens view anxiety as an all-or-nothing game—you either don't have it at all or you get flooded with intolerable discomfort. But anxious teens need to learn a different lesson—that, despite their doubts, they can indeed tolerate small to moderate amounts of anxiety as they make small changes in their behavior—that is, purposely tolerating small to moderate amounts of anxiety and experiencing the results.

You can help them learn this lesson by reframing anxiety as an experience on a scale from zero to very uncomfortable. Your teen should consider *what small change to make* that would be tolerable, in terms of the anxiety that it creates, rather than what she feels that she can't do. You can encourage her along this path by asking the right questions. For example, when your teen fearfully says, "I just can't do it," ask her, "What is something you might be able to do that would provoke less anxiety?" Often teens who are anxious will be too stuck in irrational thinking to figure this out, so you might need to help your teen identify doable steps to take.

Support Your Teen to Face Those Fears

Ultimately the best way to get rid of fears is to fully face them—the *exposure with response prevention* strategy mentioned earlier. It is the most effective of all the strategies for reducing anxiety; it works with all ages and across all types of fears. Exposure means to deliberately face a fear. Response prevention means that when facing fears, you stop trying to decrease your anxiety through avoidance or any other means—that is, with your usual responses. As discussed, continued avoidance cannot teach teens that their fears are tolerable and not as dangerous as they believe.

Avoidance can be very obvious or well hidden. It spans any tactics we use to prevent us from feeling anxious, no matter how small the change. So your teen could avoid a situation, a person, or an object. He could avoid a way of behaving or even avoid a thought. Many teens avoid situations in order to prevent the triggering of uncomfortable physical sensations. Stay open to all the ways that your teen avoids by observing his behavior when he is anxious.

Exposure changes anxious behavior, positively changes beliefs about the consequences of taking risks, and *reduces anxiety in the long run*. There is more discussion of successful ways to do exposure in Chapter 4 (for all kinds of avoidance), Chapter 5 (for social fears), and Chapter 6 (for perfectionism).

The Simple Truth About Anxiety

Strategies such as challenging negative thoughts and using exposure to confront and reduce anxiety are well-researched and successful techniques. However, successfully reducing anxiety comes down to the simple fact that to beat anxiety, we have to *do the opposite* of what it wants us to do. So if anxiety tells your teen to avoid something, your teen has to confront it instead. If it wants you to give in to your teen's avoidance, do the opposite. If it wants your teen to believe her worries, she needs to do the opposite. If it wants you and your teen to work too hard at ensuring absolute safety and certainty (which is impossible), do the opposite and encourage a little uncertainty. By not listening to anxiety or following its rules, your teen can weaken or even eliminate its impact.

3 My Constant Worrier

*Overcoming Fearful Thinking
and Repetitive Worries*

Julie's Story: A Snapshot of Worry

Julie is a bright, hardworking tenth grader, a high achiever. She gets mostly A's, takes multiple honors classes, and is captain of her lacrosse team. After getting a C-minus on a very challenging chemistry test, she later snapped at her mother over a small disagreement and became tearful. When her mother asked her what was wrong, Julie blurted out, "Mom, I am so useless. I can't do anything right. I might as well quit chemistry. I am probably going to fail the course! Who cares anyway? I am never going to get into college. I'll end up being a bag lady living on the street!"

In the days that followed, Julie was stuck in the throes of worry and could barely sleep. She felt like a total failure. She kept going over in her mind how her score meant that she wasn't good at anything and wouldn't go far. She began to worry about how she would perform on the next test and even began to contemplate what to do when she couldn't get into any good college. *I blew it*, she thought.

Understanding Worry

Does this snapshot sound like your daughter or son, spiraling into anxiety and being caught in the grip of worry? Most of us have experienced worry at one time or another in our lives, so we know what this aspect of anxiety feels like. We all must cope with a little bit of worry here and there. However, when worry gets stuck and begins to grow, it can hugely affect feelings and behavior.

The Signs of Worry

What do you notice about your anxious teen? Does he or she:

- Worry a lot of the time about a lot of different things?

- Worry intensely, out of proportion to the situation?

- Worry that something terrible is going to happen?

- Experience stomachaches or other signs of physical distress?

- Act irritable or tense due to constant worries?

- Have trouble sleeping or concentrating?

- Ask lots of "What if" questions?

- Repeatedly seek reassurance?

- Avoid situations that feel unsafe?

Teen worriers repeatedly blow events out of proportion, and in doing so, they trigger further anxiety. This anxiety can cause physical distress, which can show up in the form of stomachaches, headaches, and muscle tension. Worries intrude on day-to-day thinking, which makes it hard for teens to concentrate. Worries stop the mind from quieting down, which can keep both body and mind on high alert and trigger sleep problems. And as we've discussed, worries can make it so hard for teens to face potentially risky situations that they often completely avoid them.

The True Nature of Worry

Although people often say, "I am worried" to mean "I am feeling anxious," worry is an act of thinking, not feeling. Teen worriers think about a problem over and over in an attempt to reduce their anxiety and better cope with the problem. Worriers, being driven by their anxiety, are constantly on the lookout for danger ahead. As a result, they spend a lot of time considering all the possible ways that something could go wrong! Since they don't want to overlook or minimize any potential risks, they ask themselves and others lots of "What if" questions. All of this mental activity takes lots of effort, so it's no wonder worriers tend to become irritable and exhausted at times!

A key characteristic of worriers in general is that they try to predict future events with 100-percent certainty, so they can't tolerate not knowing for sure how something will turn out. This *intolerance of uncertainty* makes sense when we view worrying as a superhuman effort to avoid danger: any outcome that is uncertain naturally carries the possibility of danger.

Worriers cope with their need for certainty in three ways: they ask for reassurance that they are safe, they repeatedly check to see that they are safe, and they avoid taking risks whenever possible.

Worrying Is a Coping Strategy

We now suspect, based on research, that worry may actually be a form of cognitive avoidance. In other words, when they are worrying, people can avoid becoming more anxious! How can this be? Research by Tom Borkovec and his colleagues suggests that worry actually dampens emotion and can even reduce our physiological response to anxiety. Worriers feel comfort in mentally dwelling on a problem rather than fully experiencing the distressing emotions. The mental distraction may help them avoid the full impact of anxiety.

Most people use worry as a key coping strategy to try to prevent bad events from occurring, so worry gives an illusion of control. However, research shows, and we know from our own life experience, that the vast majority of things people worry about never happen. So, as the worrier overfocuses on all the ways that something could go wrong, worry ultimately heightens a sense of danger.

What Do Teens Worry About?

Much like adults, teens worry about a variety of things. In fact, anything that pertains to their basic sense of safety is a target for their worry. High up on their list of worries is whether they have performed competently in any kind of situation they are in, be it academic, social, or a talent they engage in. Many worry about core safety issues—for example, *What if a robber wants to break into my house?* Identity issues can be a source of worry during this developmental period. Some worry about their long-term future, or about dangerous world events. They also tend to worry about things that are very unlikely to occur, such as being in a plane crash.

Faulty Thinking Triggers Anxiety and Worry

Worriers believe that their fears will become true; they rarely stop to doubt the worry itself. However, anxiety can be triggered by the specific ways that we perceive situations. When we view the situation as more dangerous than it really is, these thoughts act as a foundation for worries and drive them forward.

Teens become especially prone to thinking in extremes when stress increases. Think about Julie, the anxious tenth-grader whom we met at the beginning of the chapter. Julie's thoughts spiraled out of control, ending with the dramatic outcome of her being a bag lady living on the street. I call this the "runaway worry train." Negative thoughts can quickly set off a chain reaction, leading to even more extreme thoughts—and a final catastrophic thought. The worry train is now out of control and speeding too quickly down the tracks!

The Way Teen Worriers Think

Chapter 2 introduced "thinking errors" as specific patterns of faulty thinking that can trigger anxiety (see Appendix B for a list of these errors). Adolescence—with its emphasis on identity development, tests of performance, and increased stress—can especially put teens at risk for these faulty patterns in thinking. Here are some ways that teens misperceive situations.

Fearing the Worst

Most teens when under stress tend to blow problems completely out of proportion by *catastrophizing*, a thinking error in which they not only predict a negative outcome but also assume that it will be a catastrophe when it occurs. People who catastrophize tend to make two key errors: They overestimate both the *probability* of something bad happening and the *severity* of this potential outcome. It is basically a double whammy—*the outcome I was afraid of will happen, and it will be the worst possible outcome that could happen.* Lacking the perspective gained through experience, teens often view minor setbacks as completely disastrous. And despite the fact that the final feared outcome is incredibly unlikely, their worry frequently makes them fear impending doom.

Thinking in Extremes

Many teens fall into a pattern of judging themselves in very critical and extreme ways. For example, they tend to engage in a great deal of *all-or-nothing thinking*, seeing things in extremes—all good or all bad, perfection or failure. Imagine viewing the world this way, and you can see how it might trigger anxiety. If there is nothing in between good and bad, then there is nothing in between safety and danger! Teens frequently engage in all-or-nothing thinking when facing tests of performance, which they often see as measures of their competence and worth.

Assuming a Pattern of Defeat

Overgeneralizing means taking one negative event or fact, or a few, and making too broad and negative a generalization about the future—overestimating both the severity of the problem and the danger involved. Often, teens don't have the life experience to adequately put the negative events in perspective, so they easily assume an ongoing pattern of defeat. And with their self-esteem and identity still in flux, each problem they encounter feels like too much to handle, and they magnify it to mean something terrible for their future.

Noticing Only the Negatives

Some anxious teens gravitate toward noticing everything that went wrong as opposed to what went right, an error of perception called *mental filtering*. This way of perceiving situations can trigger anxiety because it discounts positive factors that minimize danger. A teen with a tendency to worry is always on the lookout for ways that her plan will not work. In fact, she is so busy looking for problems that she doesn't even notice things that are actually working well.

Identifying Faulty Thinking

Learning to identify errors in thinking can be tricky. However, getting good at this will help you figure out when your teen's worry thoughts are picking up speed on the runaway worry train. Consider again Julie, our anxious tenth-grader. Notice that Julie is catastrophizing when she imagines becoming a bag lady just from one poor grade on a test! When Julie, a strong student and good athlete, says, "I am useless. I can't do anything right," this is an example of all-or-nothing thinking. Julie thinks that unless she performs perfectly on everything she attempts, she is a failure.

Julie is also showing a tendency to overgeneralize; that is, to draw too broad and negative a conclusion from her situation. For example, when Julie says, "I might as well quit chemistry. I am probably going to fail the course!" she is unwittingly concluding that a single event means an unending pattern of defeat.

If you were Julie's mother, you might be perplexed by Julie's assessment, knowing that Julie has never failed a course and has been getting

B's on previous chemistry tests. Julie is also not considering that the odds for getting into college are in her favor, despite a poor grade on her test. She is perceiving her situation through a mental filter and noticing only problems and risk. As Julie engages in multiple thinking errors, she ends up viewing one test as if it determines her entire destiny!

Activity: Spot Faulty Thinking

This exercise will give you more practice in spotting thinking errors. For each statement, see if you can identify which of four common thinking errors might be occurring. This will help you spot ways that your teen displays faulty thinking. A description of each error follows.

- **Overgeneralizing:** Drawing an overly broad and negative conclusion from a single situation
- **Catastrophizing:** Fearing the worst possible outcome
- **Mental filter:** Focusing only on the negatives of the situation
- **All-or-nothing thinking:** Seeing things in black and white with no middle ground

1. I performed badly on the SAT, so now I won't get into college.

2. By skipping a word of my speech, I made a fool of myself.

3. I will probably perform terribly at tryouts and then be cut from the team.

4. If I don't get a 4.0 GPA, I will disappoint everyone and be a failure.

5. I didn't do well on my audition, so I guess I am never going to be a good musician.

What type of error did you think each statement represented? It is okay if you thought of more than one for a statement. There can be overlap between the errors because they all involve focusing on the negative and jumping to the wrong conclusion. What is more important than exactly labeling the error is learning to notice that your teen is making such thinking errors. Questions 1 and 3 can be examples of catastrophizing, where one essentially fears the worst. Question 2 can be an example of mental filtering (noticing only the negatives). Question 4 can be an example of all-or-nothing thinking (assuming that without perfection, one is a failure), and Question 5 can represent overgeneralizing—taking a single incident and wrongly assuming that it indicates a pattern of bad outcomes in the future.

Activity: Listen for Faulty Thinking

When we practice analyzing thoughts, we learn to spot thinking errors more quickly over time. Now listen carefully the next time your teen talks to you during an anxious moment. Then write down in a journal statements your teen makes when he is anxious. What do you notice?

I notice that my teen tends to:

☐   View a single event as a pattern of defeat (overgeneralize)

☐   Fear the worst possible outcome (catastrophize)

☐   Notice only negatives (mental filter)

☐   Think in black-and-white extremes (all-or-nothing thinking)

☐   All of the above!

While we are noticing our teen's faulty thinking, it is also a good idea to watch for when we might make the same errors, especially when we are anxious. It may help you to write down in a journal an example of when you made a similar error.

I notice that I tend to:

☐   View a single event as a pattern of defeat (overgeneralize)

☐   Fear the worst possible outcome (catastrophize)

☐   Notice only negatives (mental filter)

☐   Think in black-and-white extremes (all-or-nothing thinking)

☐ All of the above!

Observing over time the errors that we all sometimes make in our thinking will help you to better understand the impact of faulty thinking on your and your teen's emotions. A downloadable worksheet is available at http://www.newharbinger.com/34657. (See the back of the book for more information.)

Continue to observe the type of thinking errors your teen makes when she is anxious. This will help you see the connections between her anxious thoughts, feelings, and behaviors.

Parenting Strategies to Decrease Everyday Worry

Even though it seems like teens' worries take on a life of their own, parents can exert a positive influence in helping teens tame their worries. There is a right time to get through to your teen and a right way to connect. And even though teens have to do the hard work to defeat their worries, the guidance parents can offer can go a long way toward vanquishing their fears.

Begin with Empathy

Empathy is the first step in understanding your teen's worries, because before he will let you engage with him, first and foremost he needs to feel understood. Empathy also allows you to really uncover the specific nature of the worries that your teen is experiencing.

So as Chapter 2 introduced, before you try to *correct* worries, begin by *connecting*. How can we do that effectively during an anxious moment? A good approach is to start out by reflecting back what your teen is thinking and feeling. Avoid giving advice; teens may discount your empathy and instead sense a lecture. For example, if your teen worries about a test grade (like Julie, the anxious tenth-grader), you might say, "I see that you are feeling really upset about your test. You think that a bad grade means that you are not good enough in chemistry to pass the course. And you have been trying so hard. It must feel very worrisome to think that colleges may not accept you. That is a really scary thought."

What have you just done? Entered *your teen's world.* You can help your teen only once she sees that you understand what she is going through. Otherwise, you will likely hear "You don't understand. Leave me alone!" Now, from that crucial vantage point, you can focus on modifying her perceptions.

> The first step to connecting with your anxious teen is to empathize. Avoid judging; try to briefly verbalize what she is thinking and feeling.

Choose the Right Time to Tackle Worries

During an anxious episode, teens need to change their unrealistic thinking in order to decrease their anxiety, but you can't do that for them. You can only give them guidance. When should you try? In most situations, it is better to wait until your teen *is less distressed,* since at the height of anxiety teens can become extremely irrational. So don't try to engage with your teen when she is so upset that she can't see past the clouds to the sunshine! Wait until a little time has passed and you see that she seems receptive to a discussion and ready to absorb new information.

In some teens, anxiety creates a lot of physical distress, which also acts as a feedback loop, sending a signal to their brain that they are in danger. In this state, they may not be able to discuss their thinking until they get a little calmer. Sometimes a teen just needs some extra time to decompress. Then when he is feeling calmer, you can talk with him about his thoughts.

Teach the Importance of Perceptions

To encourage teens to transform their worries, we have to start out by teaching them how important thoughts are. Through gentle discussion with your teen, you can help her learn something very important: the way we think about a situation affects how we feel. Although that is fairly obvious to adults, teens seldom consider that their feelings are based on their unique perceptions of a situation.

You can also emphasize another important fact: deliberately *changing how you think about a situation can directly change how you feel.* Thoughts are highly subjective. In fact, two teens can take the identical situation and, just by perceiving it differently, feel differently about it. For example, one teen might be devastated by receiving a 75 on a test. Another might think, *Whew, it could be worse. I was worried that I was going to fail, and in fact my average in the class is still fine.* Again, try to give a few examples from your own life to illustrate how changing the way you viewed a situation changed how you felt.

Once you have talked about the influence of thoughts on feelings, share the idea that *not all perceptions are accurate*—some are completely inaccurate and some are only partially accurate. You can use examples from your own life when you thought one thing but realized only later that because you were so upset, you were not thinking through the whole situation. Help your teen understand that when we are anxious it is useful to examine our thoughts to see how realistic they are, and that the goal is not to try to overcome negative thinking with "pie in the sky" positive thinking, but rather to replace unrealistic thoughts with more realistic thoughts.

Teach Your Teen How to Test Out Worries

To evaluate thoughts, your teen should act like a detective, seeking evidence for whether her perceptions really are true. If she thinks carefully about her circumstances, she can often come up with facts that contradict her worries. After that, it is helpful for her to evaluate her thoughts for common thinking errors, to uncover key ways in which her worries are unrealistic. Practicing this additional step will help your teen to minimize faulty thinking in the future. Here are some questions that your teen can use to evaluate her worries step by step:

Putting Worries to the Test

- What are some facts of the situation that make my thoughts not true or less true?

- What are some facts suggesting that what I think will happen may not actually occur?

- Based on these facts, what errors in thinking have I made?

  Am I overestimating how likely or severe the problem is? (Catastrophizing)

  Am I seeing the problem in black or white, nothing in between? (All-or-nothing thinking)

  Am I assuming ongoing negative outcomes without enough evidence? (Overgeneralizing)

  Am I discounting any positive events as if they don't exist? (Disqualifying the positive)

  Am I noticing only the negatives, not the positives? (Mental filter)

Once she has evaluated her worries, your teen should try to replace her worries with more realistic thoughts. Ultimately, the best way for your teen to reduce her anxiety is to get into the habit of noticing anxious thoughts as they pop up, testing out those thoughts as quickly as possible, and replacing any faulty thinking with realistic thinking. If your teen can engage in this activity when her worries begin to take hold, then you will see significant improvements in her ability to perceive situations more realistically.

The beauty of teaching your teen to analyze her thinking is that it helps minimize advice-giving, which teens often discount, especially when they are in the midst of faulty thinking. By encouraging your teen to put worries to the test, you are essentially teaching your teen *how* to think instead of teaching your teen *what* to think.

Challenge Worries with Socratic Questioning

Teens caught in the grip of anxiety often don't even notice their anxious thoughts, only their anxious feelings. In those moments, the sensations of anxiety take over, and it is hard for them to see the forest for the trees. When this occurs, parents can play an important role in helping their teen pause and consider how the way he is viewing a situation might be worsening or even causing his anxiety. As discussed in Chapter 2, the best way to do this is through Socratic questioning. Make sure your teen is not at the height of anxiety and panic when you engage with him, since in that state he won't be able to reflect on his thinking.

When your teen is calm enough to engage, gently guide him to *challenge his worries* by asking questions that target the faulty way he is viewing a situation. For example, if you notice your teen dwelling on the negative and discounting all of the positive things he has done, ask a question such as "Are you overlooking what you did well?" If your teen fears failing a test and then begins thinking his life will be over, you can ask, "Is it possible that the worst-case scenario might not happen, or could this situation be less risky or bad than you think?" These types of questions can serve many useful purposes, such as:

- Fostering calm dialogue with your teen

- Identifying worry thoughts

- Discovering facts that dispute worries

- Putting problems into perspective

- Encouraging problem-solving

- Supporting positive coping if things don't work out

Overall, these questions then serve as a powerful springboard to help your teen step back from his worries and engage in new ways of thinking and behaving. Try not to ask all of these questions all the time, though. For many teens, that may be overkill. Even one or two well-timed questions can lead your teen away from his irrational thoughts toward more realistic thinking and better coping behavior. See Appendix A for a useful list of Socratic questions that specifically elicit and then challenge all types of worries. Then, in the next exercise, try asking questions in the style of Socratic questioning. You may refer to the list in Appendix A for questions to consider.

Activity: Practice Questioning, Not Answering

For each of these anxious statements in which you spotted a thinking error, devise a question you might ask. This will help prepare you to try out Socratic questioning with your teen. There are no right or wrong answers for this exercise, as long as you practice questioning, not answering. Initially it may seem challenging, but with practice you'll get the hang of it.

1. I performed badly on the SAT, so now I won't get into college.

2. By skipping one word in my speech, I made a fool of myself.

3. I will probably perform terribly at tryouts and then be cut from the team.

4. If I don't get a 4.0 GPA, I will disappoint everyone and be a failure.

5. I didn't do well on my audition, so I guess I am not really cut out to be a musician.

Now practice trying out a Socratic question or two the next time your teen is anxious and stuck in worry. Remember to first empathize and wait until the anxiety is not at its peak.

Not all worries are unrealistic. If analyzing the worry shows that your teen is thinking realistically and not blowing a fear out of proportion, encourage a focus on coping and problem solving.

Time to Problem Solve

When your teen's worries are not based on faulty thinking—that is, there is a real and challenging problem at hand—your teen should switch to a problem-solving approach. On her own or with your help, your teen can *brainstorm all possible options* for solving a problem (without eliminating any option at first) and consider the advantages and disadvantages of each option. Then she should choose an option, no matter how imperfect, and act on it. If this is a large problem, help your teen divide it into chunks and consider strategies for addressing each part.

Sometimes teens resist a problem-solving approach because they want everything to work out perfectly. This is not always possible! Encourage your teen to try this approach even if he is not certain about the outcome. Watch out for faulty thinking during this process, because even if the problem is real, teens tend to exaggerate the depth of the problem and think that their problem-solving efforts will be futile.

Moving into a problem-solving mode shifts the emphasis away from overwhelming emotion to thinking with logic. It also can move our focus away from a future threat to the here and now. This naturally reduces anxiety, since worry always concerns the future. For example, Sarita, a sixteen-year-old, would often worry about her coach yelling at her for being late to soccer practice. One day, stuck in a bad traffic jam, the family became extremely late for an important game. Sarita became more and more distraught about what would happen when she arrived late. With encouragement from her mother, Sarita decided to call the coach to let him know she would be late. She also thought through what to say to him when she arrived. This focus on problem-solving had a small but significant effect, decreasing Sarita's anxiety in the moment.

Some teens tend to worry about problems that are far off in the future (such as whether they will get a good job after college). Again, worry often focuses on future problems that cannot be solved right away. Teens also worry about problems that are unlikely to happen in the near future and really can't even be solved (such as whether a parent will get very ill). If you notice that your teen is stuck on a problem that really is unsolvable or can't be dealt with in the near future, encourage your teen to refocus his behavior on things he can control.

> When your teen stays focused on an unproductive worry, empathize with how hard it is to let go of a worry we can't immediately or easily fix. Then gently steer him toward what is important in the here and now.

Show How You Cope with Worry

Guiding your teen to tackle persistent worries and to problem solve doesn't have to be direct. Some teens may be reluctant to engage with their parents when the subject is direct disputing of their worry. However, by just observing how parents handle stress and worry, teens can learn many things. This is the power of modeling: *showing instead of telling.*

In the presence of your teen, show how you challenge worries on the spot. Make sure not to over-accentuate the importance of worries. Instead, you can "think out loud" how some of your worries are unproductive and are best ignored. When something unexpected happens to throw you off your plan, you can demonstrate how you work to respond calmly and switch into problem-solving mode. When you exaggerate the severity of a situation (which we all sometimes do), show how you go on to put it into perspective. Don't be afraid to show your imperfections—research suggests that modeling works even better when we initially display our fears and struggles and then go on to demonstrate how we successfully cope with a challenge. It's especially useful to demonstrate ways that you take reasonable risks despite worry.

On a daily basis, by showing how you *walk your talk*—through realistically assessing problems, shaking off worry, and moving ahead with positive actions— you instill a type of learning that can have powerful effects on your teen. Without really trying, your teen can learn how to recognize and then discard worries in the moment. Worry then takes second place to living life, accepting uncertainty, and facing fears.

Overcoming Repetitive Worries

So far, we have discussed strategies for dealing with everyday worry. Yet there is another type of worry that is qualitatively different. This worry can pop into your teen's mind all on its own, without your teen's even having faulty thinking. It tends to be about very rare or impossible events, such as a parent's suddenly disappearing. Once the worry gets going, it stays stuck, repetitively signaling danger, and no amount of reassurance seems to take such a worry away.

This type of worry *plays by different rules*, so to defeat it, we have to as well! Rather than finding evidence to talk back to such a worry, it is time for your teen to see it for what it really is—a false alarm. As with any false alarm, it can make your teen nervous but it doesn't lead to danger. In this circumstance, your teen should just act as if the worry is not important, like harmless spam in her e-mail inbox. If your teen repeatedly asks for reassurance or avoids situations that seem subjectively dangerous, the worry tends to stick around longer (if this is the case, see Chapter 4 for strategies to overcome avoidance).

Gabriel's worry told him that a stranger would break into the house and kidnap him. He knew that this was extremely unlikely to happen, but the fear remained anyway. This worry would often pop into his head at night when he was tired. He would sometimes check to make sure the door was locked or ask his mother if they lived in a safe neighborhood. Reassurance didn't seem to help, because deep down he knew that this was not a realistic fear, but no one could convince him that it couldn't possibly ever happen. To overcome this worry, he labeled it as a false alarm. He then changed his behavior accordingly, by not obsessively checking the locks or getting reassurance. He expected that the fear would recur on occasion, but he stopped thinking this was a big deal when it popped into his mind. Within weeks, the intensity of the worry had subsided, and it eventually disappeared.

In Chapter 2, we discussed how suppression of anxious thoughts is a strategy that never works, but can instead make thoughts stronger. This is especially true of repetitive worries. The more your teen gets upset by a worry and then tries to stop thinking about it, the more it seems to stick around and even worsen. If she does the opposite—if she deliberately and intensely concentrates on a repetitive worry without trying to think of anything else—a surprising thing can happen. She can eventually—sometimes even quickly—become bored by the worry that she was initially afraid of!

Along those lines, when teens repeatedly seek reassurance from parents about their repetitive worries, they are engaging in a subtle form of avoidance, since they quickly get to stop thinking about the worry and reduce their anxiety. That is why, as we discussed in Chapter 2, it backfires when parents go overboard with reassurance. The next time your teen comes back to you for reassurance about a repetitive worry, remind him, "Even though you feel better when I reassure, it doesn't keep the worry away for long. So, although this is difficult, try to just allow it to be, and it will go away on its own."

Should We Accept Worries or Get Rid of Them?

The answer, surprisingly, might be both. Although there is great value in your teen's learning how to develop more realistic thinking, newer, acceptance-based models of anxiety treatment suggest that we try not to take anxious thoughts too seriously. Instead, the key is to accept the worries as just thoughts and continue to move forward, toward what is important, despite the anxiety. For example, Jay was really concerned that his dancing looked awkward to others. Despite being nervous, he decided that what was more important than listening to his anxious thoughts was trying to have some fun! So he attended the next dance and didn't give his worries too much importance. When your teen can practice this new mode of dealing with thoughts and feelings, the anxiety often naturally decreases. With this perspective, the goal is not to completely get rid of worries or anxiety but to *carry on with life* in spite of them.

Accepting worries over time will require your teen to practice getting used to uncertainty and not giving importance to the "What if" scenarios that occasionally pop up in her mind. To help your teen on this path, encourage her to continue to take reasonable risks in life, despite her worries. Ultimately, when one can accept thoughts as "just thoughts," worries become less powerful.

4 My Anxiously Avoiding Teen

Eliminating Avoidance and Learning How to Face Fears

Hannah's Story: The Cycle of Avoidance

Hannah was at school one day when a friend sitting beside her at lunch threw up. Horrified, Hannah became very fearful that she might throw up too. Soon after, she began avoiding friends at school who had been sick. She also started eating less at lunch most days, since being full made her think that she was going to throw up. Dance class then became a problem, because she didn't want to spin around or get too tired, fearing again that she would throw up. By the time her perplexed mother got wind of her fears, Hannah's life had begun to completely revolve around efforts to not throw up. She repeatedly asked her mother whether she was going to be sick, but, despite frequent reassurance and lots of avoidance, her anxiety remained. Surprised at the strength of her fears, Hannah thought, *Why am I so afraid all the time?*

All About Avoidance

Teens like Hannah are caught in the cycle of avoidance. Feeling that they must avoid something dangerous, upsetting, or unpleasant at all costs, they systematically change their behaviors, one by one, in an attempt to somehow escape what they fear. As they frantically try to fend off the feared event, previously neutral activities and situations become associated in their minds with what they fear, and so they must avoid those too. This avoidance never seems to be enough, though—as their anxiety persists and even grows, they keep looking for more ways to feel better. They don't realize it's the avoidance itself that is driving their fears.

Avoidance is one of the most destructive aspects of anxiety, and teens with all kinds of anxiety are vulnerable to it. The more a teen avoids, the more relief the teen gets from avoidance, which reinforces this behavior. Like a boulder picking up speed as it rolls down a mountain, avoidance accelerates until it can overwhelm a teen's life, making it hard to think or do much of anything else. Getting past this avoidance is the biggest challenge parents and teens face when dealing with anxiety.

Recognizing Avoidance

It is important to bear in mind that avoidance includes anything that your teen avoids confronting due to how anxious or uncomfortable it makes him or her feel. It's not simply a matter of staying away from a difficult object or situation. Avoidance can span situations, thoughts, feelings, and behaviors. Anxious teens commonly avoid

- Thoughts that trigger anxiety

- Environments or situations that trigger anxiety

- Activities that trigger anxiety

- Experiencing uncomfortable physical sensations

- "Dangerous" inanimate objects or living creatures

Avoidance can be complete or partial. Imagine being fearful of encountering a bear in the forest. Complete avoidance would entail staying out of the forest! Partial avoidance would allow entering the forest but perhaps taking a longer route that would involve less risk of encountering the bear. This partial avoidance is called a *safety behavior* because it is designed to limit the risk of confronting the feared situation and the potential impact. Safety behaviors make people feel that when a feared disaster doesn't happen, it's thanks to the influence of their safety behavior.

One powerful method of identifying even subtle avoidance is to observe your teen and notice what tends to trigger his anxiety and the ways in which he changes his behavior to cope with it.

Activity: The Way My Teen Avoids

To better understand the way that your teen avoids, ask yourself, *Is my teen avoiding…*

- Certain people, places, or events?

- Participating in activities because of something that he fears?

- The experience of anxious feelings?

- Experiencing certain physical sensations?

Now try to connect the dots in terms of how and why your teen specifically avoids. Here are a few examples:

- "When my teen does homework, he reviews it excessively to avoid making a mistake that he perceives is extremely risky."

- "When my teen won't introduce herself to someone new, she is trying to avoid even the slightest possibility of disapproval."

- "When my teen complains of a headache and skips soccer practice, he is avoiding having to experience performance anxiety."

If you are not sure why your teen is avoiding, the next time you notice his avoidance, gently ask, "What makes you want to do that?" or "In what way does avoiding this situation feel better to you?" Teens can be surprisingly insightful and honest about what is driving their behavior.

The Myths and Truths About Avoidance

Most teens don't realize the huge negative repercussions of avoidance of their fears. It seems logical to avoid what they fear—it seems to be the only thing that makes them feel better in the moment. Unfortunately, avoiding simply strengthens their belief that the situation truly is dangerous and prevents their realization that they can safely and tolerably confront it. As a coping strategy, avoidance is the worst possible trap for your teen to fall into.

Parents and teens need to learn the truth about avoidance, so that teens don't rely on it as a strategy for dealing with fears. Here, in a nutshell, are the myths and truths about avoidance:

Myths:

- Avoidance protects you from anxiety.

- Without avoidance, anxiety will soar sky-high and never come back down.

- Avoidance reduces fears.

- Avoidance is the only strategy for feeling less afraid.

Truths:

- Avoidance is not needed to protect us from anxiety, since anxiety is not harmful.

- When anxiety goes up, it never stays high forever; it always comes back down.

- Avoidance worsens fears.

- Confronting fears is a better and longer-lasting strategy for feeling less afraid.

What your teen doesn't realize is that avoidance is like jumping on a trampoline—it may make you think that you are free of anxiety and danger, but invariably you are right back where you started! To vanquish anxiety demands a new type of strategy. By reducing avoidance, teens learn that the situation is not as dangerous or uncomfortable as they thought. Through confronting fears, they also learn that *anxiety does not stay sky-high* forever but comes down naturally over time.

> Facing fears is a form of experiential learning. One learns through experience that facing fears is safe and doable and ultimately lessens anxiety.

Lay the Groundwork for Facing Fears

Once you know how avoidance backfires and makes anxiety worse, you realize that the sooner your teen begins to face her fears, the better! However, before your teen can really begin to work on new behaviors, you have to help prepare your teen for this new way of behaving. The preparation will start with you changing your own behavior, motivating your teen to change hers, and educating your teen about how to face fears.

Reward Avoidance Less

While parents can't force teens to confront anxiety-provoking situations, as a first step they can make it less easy for their teen to avoid. Children, and particularly teens, are adept at getting their parents to help them avoid. For example, a socially anxious teen may ask a parent to e-mail her teacher or speak to a coach on her behalf. A teen experiencing panic may request that his parent accompany him to events in order to decrease his anxiety. Anxious teens may also push for family routines to be modified to allow for easier avoidance.

In an empathetic way, let your teen know that in order to help him *overcome his anxiety*, you won't continue to help him *avoid what he fears*. Reducing the ways in which you accommodate your child's avoidance will reduce how much avoidant behavior is rewarded and help your teen learn to cope with his fears.

You can also use the strategy of attending to non-anxious behavior, described in Chapter 2. Parents often get into battles with their teens when avoidance flares up. This can unwittingly give attention to and reward avoidance as a behavior. Although this may surprise you, too much focus on advice-giving during times of avoidance can also unintentionally give the avoidance a great deal of attention. Instead, *ignore negative behavior* and *acknowledge each positive change* in behavior.

Activity: My Beliefs About Anxiety and Avoidance

Many parents understand the dangers of avoidance quite logically, but emotionally they do not like to see their children suffer. They see that confronting fears can be quite difficult and very distressing. Some parents also worry that pushing their teen to experience anxiety might make things worse. Before you commit to an approach that reduces avoidance, ask yourself whether you might have your own beliefs about anxiety that could sneak in and impede your plans to reduce it. Here are some questions to consider:

- Do I think that experiencing anxiety by facing her fears is harmful for my teen?

- Do I worry that my teen will be unable to cope with his anxiety when facing his fears?

- Do I feel bad as a parent for intentionally making my teen suffer by pushing her to face her fears?

Give these questions some careful thought, even if you initially answer "no." You need to address your own fears about your teen's reducing avoidance before you can effectively respond to that avoidance. It may be helpful to write down your answers in a journal. What might you discover?

Increase Your Teen's Motivation for Change

Most teens, even if they want to confront their fears, feel that it is just too hard to do. Parents need to help them see that it is worth it to confront their fears. A good way to encourage teens to see the light is to ask them some questions designed to instill in them both *the need for change* and *the hope that they indeed can change*. You can ask questions such as these:

- In what way has anxiety gotten in the way of your doing things that you really want to do?

- How much of your life has the anxiety taken over?

- How will you be able to behave differently when your anxiety decreases?

- What can you imagine feeling and accomplishing when the anxiety decreases?

- How will your life be more joyful when you face your fears?

- What would be fun to try if you were not so anxious?

- What new challenge would you be able to try if you felt better?

Remember that when your teen takes steps to face her fears, you should positively acknowledge her effort. A simple "I notice that you…" or "I can see that you pushed yourself to…" will help your teen feel that her efforts are being recognized. Concrete rewards also can help improve motivation; the reward should be something teens have requested and set up with their parents in advance. For example, one teen earned money toward concert tickets for her favorite band by getting cash in exchange for the difficult practice that she was doing. Another teen earned the ability to download a low-cost app or song when a challenging task was completed.

Encourage Your Teen to Stop Listening to Fears

For your teen to be prepared to face his fears, it's important for him to practice interacting with anxiety in a different way. Rather than letting anxiety control him, the goal is for him to show anxiety who is *in charge*. In Chapter 2, we introduced two techniques ("Team Up with Your Teen" and "Externalize the Anxiety and Talk Back to It") that are especially useful in establishing a new way of interacting with anxiety.

First, by teaming up with your teen in a united front, you provide the support to help challenge anxiety and at the same time decrease a power struggle between you about his behavior. The degree to which you step in and support him depends on the age of your teen, your relationship with him, and how much he desires independence. Tread gently so that you can gauge his response to your efforts. To get your teen on board with your partnering, be careful not to make it about what *you* want versus what *he* wants. For example, you can say, "It looks like anxiety has gotten you stuck. How can I help support you to do the things that you really want to do?" Many teens don't mind some support if it's given in a way that allows them to lead rather than follow.

Second, by externalizing anxiety as a force that must be confronted, you help your teen to talk back to his fears. By talking back to the anxiety, he becomes more able to defeat it. If he is receptive, you can even help him talk back to anxiety the next time it triggers avoidance. Here are some examples of how your teen, by talking back to anxiety, can begin to reduce his avoidance and get ready to face his fears.

- "Hey, fears. Stop tricking me. I don't have to avoid this just because you tell me to."

- "I don't feel better when I listen to you, so I will ignore you and do the opposite."

- "Give me a break. There is no emergency, even though you tell me there is."

Explain a Powerful Method for Conquering Fears

Explain to your teen that in order to conquer fears, we have to do the opposite of what our instincts tell us to do—go toward the "danger" rather than flee from it. When we do this, our anxiety surprisingly diminishes over time. Explain that this is the basis of exposure with response prevention (introduced in Chapter 2), which research shows overcomes a wide range of fears. Let her know that *exposure* means to face what she is anxiously avoiding, and *response prevention* means to not do anything to try to banish her fear. Tell her that by confronting fears, we learn that what we were avoiding is not as bad or as dangerous as we thought, and anxiety really does come down over time.

Now, most likely your teen will initially balk at the idea that she will feel better when she confronts her fears. To help make your point, you can explain one theory of why exposure works to decrease anxiety: when we stay in a new situation long enough, we simply get used to it. It's helpful to ask, "Why do we feel less cold a few minutes after we jump into a cold pool?" Your teen will typically respond, "Because we get used to it." Explain that we can do the same thing with fears, just by staying in the situation long enough. Your teen might appreciate the metaphor of getting used to a scary movie. At first she watches it in horror, but on the third or fourth viewing, she might even be yawning at the worst part. Your teen needs to accept that she must actually experience discomfort and anxiety in order to get used to it and successfully reduce it over time. That is the counterintuitive way of beating fears.

Decide Whether You Will Be a Coach

Before your teen begins exposure, it's important to consider whether you will help him in the process of his facing his fears. This partnership can be very beneficial. As a coach, you can help your teen pick targets for exposure, encourage him to stay in a challenging situation, and praise him for the progress he makes. Whenever the chance arises, you can also model how to perform a challenging behavior.

There are circumstances, however, in which it's not a good idea to coach your teen. Some teens value their independence, want their privacy, and prefer to do the hard work on their own. You may also feel that you are too close to the situation to be an effective coach. In both cases, you can still act as your teen's cheerleader and, as your teen practices new behaviors, provide encouragement from a respectful distance. Even if you and your teen feel that coaching makes sense, it is important to step back and think about whether you can take on this often-challenging role. Before you consider coaching your teen in this area, consider whether you can

- Be patient through the sometimes slow progress and occasional setbacks

- Tolerate seeing your teen visibly distressed

- Resist stepping in with your own reassurance

- Redirect when your teen seeks reassurance

- Resist checking whether your teen is okay

- Be optimistic and positive about progress, no matter how small

Parents who have demonstrated these characteristics and behaviors have been able to provide valuable support to teens facing difficult exposures.

Enhancing Successful Exposures

Now that you have laid the groundwork for your teen to confront his fears, it is important to learn ways to maximize success, before exposures begin. When your teen embarks on the journey of challenging fears, he can run into many common obstacles. This section offers some effective strategies to sidestep or overcome them.

Choose the Right Goal

The hardest part of change is taking the first step. In the case of facing fears, successful initial practice, based on setting realistic and specific goals, is important in promoting further progress. A goal should be based on your teen's own *fear profile*—what specifically triggers your teen's anxiety. Second, your teen should choose an exposure goal that will trigger only a mild to moderate amount of anxiety at most, rather than overwhelming fear. For example, a teen afraid of social situations might have to start with practicing the smaller goal of speaking to someone new, well before speaking up in a crowd. Accomplishing the first goal will support tackling the next one. If you are serving as a coach, you can help guide your teen to choose a reasonable goal: one that is not so easy that it doesn't challenge your teen, and not so difficult that it makes exposures too hard to tolerate.

Parents have to be careful not to step in and set goals for their teens. At this developmental stage, teens should decide for themselves what behavioral goal they can begin working on. Often parents suggest goals that are well intentioned, but too difficult and better tackled after some easier practice. For example, a parent of a teen experiencing a fear of heights might say, "Come out on the balcony. You can see that it is not so bad." That teen might feel an overwhelming level of anxiety that could prevent her from staying on the balcony long enough to indeed see that it was not so bad. So she might need to start with an easier task and move up to the more daunting one.

Ask your teen what she would like to work on that is doable and not too anxiety-provoking. Picking the right goal will increase the chances of success.

Encourage Your Teen to Tolerate Uncertainty

The journey from being anxious and avoiding to feeling calm and facing your fears involves traveling through the *land of uncertainty*. There is no way around it. You can't go over or under it, only through it. As your teen begins to face fears, he may feel that nothing seems safe or certain. Despite this, he must deliberately and bravely move forward, not knowing how everything will turn out.

For example, a perfectionistic teen who is just learning how to not be so perfectionistic will wonder if something terrible will befall her when she takes that risk. Many teens will turn to their family at this time for extra reassurance. However, when your teen is facing fears, you can't jump in with continual reassurance that nothing bad will happen; that defeats the purpose of your teen's learning this for herself. Start by saying something like, "It is so hard to not completely know if everything will work out. You have to keep moving to face this challenge even though you're feeling unsure." Ultimately, your teen will do best when she can learn to embrace uncertainty and see that taking reasonable risks is a normal part of life.

> To successfully challenge fears, your teen has to tolerate the uncertainty of not knowing for sure whether something bad will happen.

Gradually Eliminate Safety Behaviors

To effectively do exposure, it is important to eliminate all kinds of safety behaviors because, again, they are a form of *partial avoidance*. This can happen gradually, but the goal is to completely eliminate them over time. Otherwise these behaviors can ruin the effectiveness of exposures. Here are some examples of safety behaviors:

- Checking over and over whether something is safe

- Engaging in too much distraction when confronting a feared situation

- Asking for reassurance when confronting a feared situation

- Staying close to something or someone who is considered safe

- Holding back from fully experiencing a feared object or situation

To discover safety behaviors during exposure, ask your teen, "When you are around what you fear, are there ways that you try to make yourself feel less upset or do something to feel more safe?" When your teen confronts situations that seem threatening, make sure that you yourself don't bring on a safety behavior by excessively reassuring him that he will be safe, which prevents him from learning this for himself.

Practice Enough to Change Beliefs About Danger

Your teen's beliefs about danger help to sustain anxiety, and they are not easily changed. People who accidentally or too briefly face a fear often try to escape the situation as quickly as possible—which can heighten the sense of danger. As well, most fears must be *faced until the situation feels more tolerable*. This means that we have to stay in a scary situation until the fear decreases and then do this repeatedly, not just once or twice. This is especially true if the fear is strong or applies to a wide range of situations.

If he faces fears in only one specific situation, your teen might think he was just lucky that nothing bad happened. To really change his beliefs, usually your teen must face them across a variety of situations. For example, if a socially anxious teen decides to attend a party and nothing bad happens, he might think that it was because of the particular people who were there. To quell his exaggerated fears of social disapproval, he needs to confront a wide variety of social situations. By doing so, he would eventually realize that his fears were either mistaken or way too extreme.

Exposures must be done

- On purpose

- Frequently enough; ideally, once a day

- For long enough each time to fully confront the fear

- Across enough different situations to really test out fears

> Anxiety goes down when your teen has fully tested out beliefs about danger multiple times and across multiple situations.

The Face-Your-Fears Plan

Once you and your teen have set the stage for change and learned the principles for effective exposure, your teen can begin to systematically confront her fears, with a step-by-step plan.

Identify and Rate Fearful Situations

Start by asking your teen to list a variety of situations that trigger her anxiety, describing each situation as clearly as possible. Then have her rate how much anxiety would be triggered if she had to face each situation. In this case, anxiety is measured on the range shown here, from 0 (not nervous) to 50 (moderately anxious) up to 100 (terrified). Your teen rates each anxiety-provoking situation on this scale. To identify a range of fears to face from mild to severe, prompt her to rank her anxiety by asking, "What would trigger a 50 level of anxiety on this scale?" For example, a socially anxious teen might say, "I would have to tell a joke to someone I don't know so well." And so on. If your teen prefers to rate her anxiety from 1 to 10 or using some other scale, that is fine, as long as she has an easy, consistent way to quantify her anxiety.

Rating My Anxiety

Fear Description	Rating
Terrified, out of control	100
	90
Really scared, almost panicked	80
	70
	60
Moderately anxious, but I can handle it	50
	40
Nervous	30
	20
Very slightly nervous—no big deal	10
Not anxious	0

Some teens who are especially sensitive to being anxious rate every situation as inducing an 80 or higher level of anxiety. If your teen finds it hard to come up with situations that trigger only a mild level of anxiety, ask, "What would make the situation less anxiety-provoking?" and then use those easier situations for this exercise. For example, a teen with a bug phobia rated being within one foot of a bug as 90 out of 100. But when asked "How can we make being within one foot of a bug easier?" he came up with "Being within one foot of a bug while I am wearing my shoes." If your teen has a problem coming up with an easier task, you could suggest one, based on what you know about his fears. A downloadable worksheet for rating anxious situations is available at http://www.newharbinger.com/34657. (See the back of the book for more information.)

For teens who have trouble coming up with a list of anxiety-provoking situations, ask, "What situations or circumstances do you frequently avoid or try to avoid?" Then use those situations to design exposure tasks.

Beyond using these ratings to devise a plan to face fears, there is a major advantage to breaking down fears in this way. Your teen will see that anxiety is not an all-or-nothing matter; rather, it's a response to a spectrum of situations, from less anxiety-provoking to more anxiety-provoking. Most teens and anxious individuals in general see anxiety-provoking situations as completely overwhelming. As they experience exposure with response prevention, they can get used to seeing distress as varying along a continuum that allows them to gradually face it, which will increase their sense of control over it.

Create a Challenge Ladder and Begin Exposures

Once your teen has a good handle on the different levels of anxiety she experiences in different circumstances, she should create a challenge ladder by ranking each item in order, from easiest to most difficult, as described shortly. Usually about eight to ten challenges are enough to make significant progress in facing a fear (sometimes even fewer steps are necessary). More steps can be added if going from one situation to the next suddenly seems too difficult. If so, she can add a challenge that is a little less anxiety provoking. She should do the steps until she feels comfortable with the behavior and her anxiety drops. A downloadable worksheet is available at http://www.newharbinger.com /34657. (See the back of the book for more information.)

Next, it is time to begin facing fears, beginning with the easiest task and moving on to increasingly difficult tasks. At each step, your teen must stay in the situation until she can tolerate her anxiety and learn that she can cope with the situation. This is called *graded exposure*—you gradually face one fearful situation at a time, experience success by seeing the anxiety decrease, and then move on to the next one. If providing concrete rewards, don't forget to give a reward after each successful exposure.

Remember Hannah, whom we met at the beginning of the chapter? Hannah worked with her mother and me to figure out all the ways that she was avoiding a situation due to her anxiety. Then she set about to reverse the cycle of avoidance. Here is an example of a piece of her challenge ladder that she helped design and then repeatedly practiced:

- Attend dance class and deliberately spin around.

- Watch a movie clip or home video on YouTube of someone throwing up.

- Eat all of my lunch at school even when I feel nervous.

- Hug a friend who has recently been sick.

Here are a few basics to keep in mind when your teen completes her challenge ladder:

- Starting with too difficult an exposure will increase the chance of failure, since high anxiety spurs people to try to escape the situation instead of tolerating it.

- Usually, when we stay in the situation, the anxiety subsides; however, this is not a requirement for a successful exposure. Typically, anxiety most often decreases much faster than people expect; however, sometimes multiple exposures are necessary over time for anxiety to decrease.

- Ideally, your teen should proceed step by step up the challenge ladder to the most fearsome situation. If the worst fear is not confronted, often thoughts about danger remain.

- Just like in real life, we don't use exposure for situations of high risk; instead, we choose to confront situations that involve reasonable, everyday levels of risk. This typically involves situations that everyone might occasionally confront and tolerate.

Activity: My Teen's Challenge Ladder

Let's practice your understanding of your teen's fear profile and create a challenge ladder to address it. Check off each step as you do it.

☐　　My teen has listed the range of situations that trigger anxiety.

☐　　My teen has rated these situations from 0 to 100 in terms of how anxiety-provoking each circumstance or situation is.

☐　　My teen has come up with a Challenge Ladder ranked from easiest to most difficult.

☐　　My teen has begun to face his fears, starting with a task that feels only mildly to moderately anxiety provoking.

The Wrap-Up

Just like having a post-game wrap-up, after teens have gradually and successfully faced their fears, it is important for them to examine what happened. Remember that practicing facing fears is meant to instill *new learning through experience*. So what we really want to see is whether, through experience with facing her fears, your teen now expects something different from before. It is also useful to check whether your teen feels better able to cope with the experience of anxiety as well. Here are some good questions to ask:

- Did you learn that the situation was less dangerous, upsetting, or unpleasant than you thought?

- Did you learn that the bad thing that you expected to happen didn't occur?

- Did you learn that you could tolerate anxiety and that it decreased over time?

- Did you learn that you could cope in the moment better than you imagined?

- Were you surprised by your ability to fully face your fears?

Through repeatedly facing their fears, teens typically learn that anxiety does not continually increase but is less powerful and long lasting than they believe. They realize that they can cope with difficult situations, and that these are not as bad as they feared. Most important, they now understand how to use this effective strategy to reduce anxiety, whether they are dealing with their current anxiety or a new worry in the future.

Here is an easy acronym that will help your teen to remember the plan:

The FACE Your Fears Plan

Face your fears one step at a time.

Accept feelings of anxiety, discomfort, and uncertainty.

Continue facing each situation until the discomfort decreases.

Experience reduced anxiety and better coping.

Challenges for a Variety of Fears

Here are a few examples of what might go on a challenge ladder to address different fears. These are challenge ladders that teens helped to design themselves, based on what uniquely felt challenging to them. In each case, the ladder was devised by figuring out what was feared and what was being avoided. Remember that your teen must create her own challenge ladder, since the particular triggers of her fear and specific ways that she responds to those fears are unique to her.

Facing My Fear

Perfectionism About Academic Performance

Edit work twice versus four times	30
Deliberately make small "mistakes" on a project	50
Deliberately write "sloppily" on a math test	80

Social Fears

At lunch, start a conversation with someone I know well	30
Introduce myself to someone I don't know well	50
Crack a joke in front of the class	80

Bug Phobia

Remain within a room's length from a bug	30
Remain within two feet of a bug	50
Tolerate holding or touching a bug	80

Separation Anxiety (about being away from a parent)

Go upstairs to get items from my bedroom alone	30
Stay upstairs alone for an hour	50
Attend a sleepover at a friend's house	80

Obsessive Fear of Germs

Wash hands up to the wrists with soap only once	30
Touch doorknobs and don't wash hands	50
Touch "dirtiest spot" and don't wash hands	80

Fear of Throwing Up

Talk about someone else throwing up	30
See a video of someone throwing up	50
Eat the same meal I ate before I last threw up	80

How Do We Know Exposure Has Worked?

The standard to judge success is not whether all anxiety has been completely eliminated, which might be too tall an order and is not necessary; rather, it is whether anxiety is no longer getting in the way of life. Ideally we want teens who chronically avoid to realize that they have repeatedly overestimated the *dangers* in their environment and underestimated *their ability to cope*. By realizing this, they will feel empowered to continue to face new situations that feel potentially risky to them. Gaining confidence in being able to cope with difficult situations is thought to play an important role in preventing future anxiety. Ask yourself:

- Is my teen's anxiety now decreased to milder, manageable levels?

- Has my teen reduced his excessive beliefs about danger?

- Is my teen no longer avoiding, but pushing herself to face fears?

- Has my teen's confidence in facing new challenging situations improved?

When your teen really embraces this model for facing fears, he will naturally be inclined to stop avoiding what he fears and instead seek new and meaningful ways of interacting with the world, which is a much better journey to be on.

5 My Socially Fearful Teen

Reducing Social Fears and Facing Social Challenges

Robert's Story: Avoiding Embarrassment

Robert, an eighth-grader, rushed down the hallway, hoping to make it to his first class on time. He worried that if he was late, everyone would stare at him. Managing to make it before the door shut, he slouched down in his seat. It was his social studies class, the one where the teacher picked people randomly to answer a question. When Robert was forced to give an answer, he thought the girl next to him gave him a funny look. She must have thought his answer was dumb. Then at lunch, he heard someone telling a joke and wanted to follow up with a retort, but fearing that it was a boring thing to say, he stayed silent. In the afternoon his anxiety got worse when he gave an oral report. He imagined that everyone noticed his voice shaking and his face turning red. Later, at the school dance, he didn't talk to anyone and left early, thinking *Epic fail! I might as well stay home next time.*

Understanding Social Anxiety in Teens

Teens like Robert are in the clutches of social anxiety, fearing that they will say or do something that will make them look completely foolish. As a result, the social landscape feels so filled with danger that they will avoid as many social situations as possible. If they have to directly face such situations, such as having to give a presentation, they will often feel acute anxiety even to the point of experiencing panic symptoms, such as rapid breathing or trembling.

What do you notice about your anxious teen? Does he or she:

- Worry about answering questions in class?

- Avoid or fear asking a teacher for help?

- Avoid social events such as parties?

- Act preoccupied with how she appears to others?

- Stay quiet in a crowd due to anxiety?

- Avoid or fear meeting new people?

- Avoid or get extremely anxious during public speaking or performances?

- Worry about how a performance will look to others?

All of these problems are aspects of how social anxiety can manifest in teens. At its core, social anxiety is a *strong fear of disapproval*. And once this fear takes hold, it greatly changes how teens act. They avoid any chance of behaving "foolishly," such as answering a question incorrectly in class, trying out for a school play, or even engaging in everyday conversation. Most importantly, social anxiety stops teens from doing what they really want to do. Instead, their whole life revolves around not making any social mistakes.

To identify possible areas of social anxiety in your teen, ask yourself, *Which social situations does he try his best to avoid? What kinds of situations create concern about how others perceive him?*

Activity: Is My Teen Just Shy or Socially Anxious?

Most parents of shy teens want to know if their teen's shyness is a sign of social anxiety. Shyness is a temperamental style that is most likely inborn. There is some evidence that shyness is related to social anxiety disorder. For example, research by psychiatrist Carl Schwartz and his colleagues found that being inhibited in early childhood when encountering new people or situations was associated with social anxiety in the teen years. On the whole, research suggests that the disorder can develop from a history of shyness or inhibition; however, being shy doesn't automatically mean your teen has social anxiety or will develop it.

Answer the following questions to get a sense of whether your teen is naturally shy or socially anxious.

1. My teen has always been a little reluctant to meet new people.   Y / N

2. My teen sometimes prefers being alone.   Y / N

3. My teen gets very worried when giving a performance.   Y / N

4. My teen always tries to avoid attention.   Y / N

5. My teen tries to avoid behaving awkwardly.   Y / N

6. My teen has always been the quiet one.   Y / N

If you answered yes to questions 3, 4, and 5, your teen may be not just shy but rather socially anxious. Answering yes to the other questions suggests a temperamental style that is likely not a problem unless it begins to involve a lot of avoidance or distress.

The Teen Years Are a Time of Social Insecurity

The developmental nature of adolescence, with its tenuous sense of identity, primes a teen for social insecurity. Teens want to fit in and not appear different. Teens also feel pressure to perform well in a variety of public situations, such as playing team sports and being part of a social group. For most teens, their social anxiety doesn't cause significant trouble and can abate gradually over time. Unfortunately, for some the fear becomes so severe that it causes both distress and dysfunction in their lives.

Most worrisome, social anxiety gets in the way of teens' accomplishing a major task of adolescence—exploring their sense of self and forging a stronger identity. Think about how much you have learned about yourself by engaging in social situations when you were a teen. Social anxiety gets in the way of practicing important developmental tasks such as making new friends, trying out a new skill, asking for help when needed, and learning to state one's opinions in a crowd. Even if your teen doesn't have severe social anxiety, any anxiety that impedes him in his development can have a growing negative impact.

The Spotlight Is on Your Teen

To socially fearful teens, the spotlight is always on them! Imagine if wherever you went, a spotlight followed you and became especially larger and brighter when you made a social faux pas. That is the way socially anxious teens feel. They think that everyone is constantly observing them and noticing their faults. To Robert, our socially anxious teen who tries desperately to avoid being late for class, all eyes are on him! He can't even fathom that his peers wouldn't consider it embarrassing for him to be two minutes late to class. Another very salient problem, which Robert's story also demonstrates, is that socially anxious teens believe that everyone notices how anxious they are, which feels even more embarrassing. Socially anxious teens particularly fear that others notice their physical signs of anxiety, such as when they tremble, shake, or blush.

Here are some fearful thoughts that illustrate this feeling of being in the spotlight:

- *If I give a wrong answer in class, everyone will notice and think I am not smart.*

- *If I ask her out, she will hear my voice tremble.*

- *If I give a presentation, people will see that I hesitated a lot and looked nervous.*

As a result of this intense fear of evaluation, these teens constantly review their performance, searching for ways that their behavior could be viewed negatively. They scan for threats and perceive even neutral situations as threatening. This is an internal threat detector gone haywire—it is set to sound the alarm too easily and too often!

Research suggests that socially anxious people pay attention to signs of threat, whereas less socially anxious people pay attention to positive evaluation.

Negative Thoughts Trigger Social Anxiety

There are some key ways in which socially anxious teens perceive social situations that trigger anxiety. First, they tend to engage in the thinking error of mind reading, making guesses about what someone else is thinking about them. Unfortunately, socially anxious teens make the assumption that people are thinking negative things about them. Yet often the evidence for their fears is either completely lacking or over-magnified. For example, imagine if someone you know walked by you in a crowd and didn't say hello. You might think, *Perhaps he was rushed and didn't notice me.* A socially anxious teen might mind read and jump to the conclusion, *He thinks I am so uncool that he doesn't even want to say hello.*

Socially anxious teens also engage in other thinking errors. When they evaluate their performance, they can't see anything except either perfection or failure—all-or-nothing thinking. So they often feel that they performed terribly, despite positive aspects of their performance. Lastly, they overestimate both the *probability* that social disapproval will happen and the *severity* of that disapproval. In other words, they think that people will notice them doing something embarrassing, and when they do, it will result in the worst possible outcome. For example, if they make a social blunder, they expect to be laughed at and completely ostracized.

Avoidance Fuels Social Anxiety

A major way that social anxiety gets rolling is through avoidance of social situations. Anxious teens begin to feel so uncomfortable in socially demanding situations that they naturally avoid them as much as possible. This avoidance produces such a feeling of relief that it is hard to get teens out of this rut. They may avoid speaking up in class, introducing themselves to strangers, or taking any new social risks.

The problem with all of this avoidance is that *flawed beliefs never get tested out as untrue.* So anxious teens never learn well enough that others really won't reject their behavior or performance, or even that some mild disapproval is okay. Over time, they lose their confidence for taking social risks. As a result, they never get used to coping with anxiety-provoking situations or engaging in productive problem solving, so their anxiety stays high.

Worst of all, avoidant teens can appear aloof to their peers, who may judge them as disengaged or even unfriendly rather than anxious. Thus they are often ignored or avoided by their peers, or at times downright rejected, which serves only to confirm their belief that their peers do not like them. It is a terrible misunderstanding with huge repercussions. The solution then is to not avoid but instead begin to face social fears. We'll see later how that's done.

Reassurance Doesn't Take Away Social Fears

Most parents, when seeing their teens stuck in the throes of anxiety about a social situation, tell them that it won't be so bad. Unfortunately, teens don't usually respond to positive predictions and reassurance about how a social situation will go for them. Their worries are so loud, it is like a drum constantly beating in their mind, drowning out everything else. If you say, "I am sure your presentation will go really well," your teen will probably think, *Mom doesn't realize that people will notice my shaking during the presentation and think I am lame.* Teens also don't feel better when you just tell them to behave positively. Their worries have a much greater influence on their behavior.

Is Social Anxiety Caused by Poor Social Skills?

You might be wondering whether social anxiety has anything to do with how socially skilled a person is. Being socially skilled means knowing how to do all the appropriate social behaviors, such as asking a question, maintaining a conversation, and giving good eye contact. Research confirms that social anxiety is not related to how socially skilled a person is; rather, those with social anxiety *think* they have inadequate social skills. This lends even more credence to the idea that social anxiety is a problem of perception. Even if your teen has good social skills, advance practicing of some behaviors, such as how to initiate and maintain a conversation at a party, can be very helpful to decrease anxiety. It will increase a sense of control over the situation and make it easier to take a risk.

If your teen seems to have a genuine problem with social skills, it is very important for him to first work on improving his social skills before he practices facing socially challenging situations. Otherwise, he is likely to experience real and continued social disapproval. Once he is making some improvements, continuing to face socially challenging situations will help him maintain and bolster his skills.

Positive Parenting Steps to Modify Anxious Perceptions

There are a number of steps parents can take to help teens view their social situations less fearfully. All rely on parents' using Socratic questioning to identify and challenge the specific irrational thoughts teens are having about their social situation. Parents can even use such questioning to challenge long-standing beliefs that contribute to the teen's social anxiety. The advantage to using such questions is that teens tend to accept them more readily than advice, and parents can use them spontaneously to steer an anxious teen's thoughts in the right direction.

Help Your Teen Identify Social Fears

To address the fearful thinking that drives social anxiety, you must first help your teen notice these bothersome thoughts. You do this by asking questions like these, which will spur your teen to identify specific worries:

- What would happen if people noticed that you did something wrong?

- What do you worry that people are thinking about you?

- What do you imagine or picture happening to you in this situation?

Keep in mind that worries can also arise in the form of mental images. For example, your teen might get a clear mental picture of social disapproval. This happened for a teen client of mine, who both imagined and saw herself in a situation where everyone pointed and laughed at her. Listen for both specific thoughts and mental imagery to get a full understanding of your teen's fears. Then it is time to help your teen challenge those fears.

Help Your Teen View Social Situations Differently

When teens have exaggerated fears of danger in social situations, they avoid taking risks. As any parent of a socially anxious teen knows, no matter how much you coax, it is challenging to get your teen to see that these fears are unfounded. Again, the best way to accomplish this is not through telling, but through asking. By *asking pointed questions*, you guide your teen to both notice and challenge anxious thoughts. Here are some questions to change the way your teen is viewing a social situation:

- Is it necessary to perform perfectly, or could it be that people aren't expecting that?

- Could your worries be exaggerating how foolish you might look?

- Could you be magnifying the importance of this one event for how others might view you?

- Is there a possibility that people will not be watching you as closely as you think?

You don't need to use all of these questions, and you might need to slightly revise them depending on the social situation, but you get the gist. Questions help your teen begin to challenge the negative thinking that gave rise to these fears.

To start to challenge social fears, teens can fill in the blanks in the following question: "Even if I fear _____, it is not likely to happen, because _____, and it is not so bad, because _____."

Help Your Teen View a Performance Realistically

Once a performance is over, socially anxious teens critically judge their performance and guess that others view them poorly as well. This includes any performance, no matter how large or small, including engaging in everyday conversation, which really feels like a performance to a socially anxious teen! The problem with this self-criticism is that it serves only to confirm an anxious teen's irrational beliefs—that she acted foolishly, and everyone thought so. Here are some questions to help your teen talk back to her worry that she made a social blunder:

- Could it be that you acted less foolishly than you thought?

- Is it possible that people didn't think you acted in an embarrassing way?

- Could people have even liked something about the way you behaved?

The goal of this questioning is for teens to get into the habit of first thinking about their fearful thoughts and realize that their thoughts are only one way of looking at the situation. Then they can come up with an *alternative way* to view the situation—not necessarily all positive—that is realistic and believable to them. This is important, because an anxious teen will readily discount completely positive and unrealistic thinking.

Identify Long-Standing Beliefs

Dysfunctional beliefs are the engine that drives anxious, irrational thoughts. Such enduring beliefs color all your teen's perceptions of potentially socially disapproving situations. For example, perfectionism—the belief that it is unacceptable to perform less than flawlessly—runs rampant in socially anxious teens. (Chapter 6 will help you better understand perfectionism.) You can also listen closely when your teen identifies his anxious thoughts to get a sense of his *underlying core beliefs* about himself. Most dysfunctional beliefs involve overly rigid rules regarding behavior. Does your teen feel everyone must approve of him at all times? If the belief colors a variety of thoughts and situations, you have hit on a dysfunctional core belief. Here are some dysfunctional beliefs socially fearful teens have expressed:

- I don't do anything right.

- I am the most boring person in this world.

- People will reject me if I don't do things perfectly every time.

- People are watching to see if I make any mistakes.

You can further probe for core beliefs by asking about the meaning of situations. For example, when your teen expresses a fearful thought, you can ask "And that would mean?" Sometimes, to get to a core belief, you have to repeatedly ask about the meaning of a situation until you get to the heart of the matter. For example, when James was asked what it would mean if he didn't get a date for a prom, he first said, "I will be the only one without a date." With the further prodding of "and not getting a date means…?" he ended up saying, "That means that I am a complete loser." Asking questions about the meaning of situations is like peeling layers of an onion. Eventually teens will express the core beliefs they truly hold.

Create More Healthy Beliefs

Teens can overcome their dysfunctional beliefs and expectations by weighing evidence from their own lives that helps counter the negative beliefs. If you catch your teen expressing such beliefs, here are some questions that will help steer him to develop more constructive beliefs about himself and the world:

- Would your friend have the same negative opinion of you as you do of yourself?

- What are some experiences that actually contradict your beliefs about yourself?

- Are there people in the world who are not as judgmental as you think?

Adolescence, being a time of social insecurity, encourages teens to think that everyone is looking at them and always judging them. This belief will be a hard one to budge, but you can take a stab at explaining how this belief is false. One way to help your teen to see the fallacy of this belief is to ask her, "Were you judging the whole time how your friend acted and whether she made even the slightest mistake?" Your teen would most likely say, "Of course not!" You then can say, "Do you see how your belief that everyone is judging you critically all the time might be too extreme?"

Core beliefs, since they have often been built up over a range of experiences, are not easily changed. However, through your gradually, gently prodding your teen with these types of questions, she will have opportunities to revise her beliefs. Don't forget that, as a parent, you have tremendous influence over your child's overall belief system. So gently nudge your teen to view herself less critically over time.

Normalize Fears and Mistakes

One basic problem for socially fearful teens is that they think they are different from everyone else. Although socially anxious teens have more frequent and severe fears than a typical teen, they need to know how common it is to be fearful in different social situations. Explain that *everyone* gets a little nervous before making a speech, giving a performance, or meeting someone new. Since socially anxious teens are afraid of others' noticing that they are afraid, help them to see it is expected that people will sometimes act nervous and appear visibly nervous (for example, by blushing).

Many teens may also not realize how common it is for people to make small social mistakes. Stumbling over a word in a speech, forgetting someone's name, or telling a joke that isn't that funny—we all act imperfectly and in a way that's all too human at times. By showing your teen that his mistakes are not so rare or different from anyone else's, you will help him revise his beliefs about himself.

Positive Parenting Steps to Modify Fearful Behavior

Once you have invited your teen to question exaggerated and unfounded perceptions about social situations, it is important to lay the groundwork for reducing avoidance and encouraging positive social behavior. Then, when your teen is better prepared, she'll need to gradually face more difficult social situations to truly overcome her anxiety.

Prevent Panic

Sometimes teens experience lots of physical symptoms of panic and anxiety, such as dizziness and shakiness, when they confront social situations. Before we push them to try out challenges, we should give them a few tools to decrease their physical anxiety. Chapter 8 discusses some good ways to reduce physical distress. For example, belly breathing can help reduce or prevent the rapid breathing that often happens with panic. Learning a few ways to decrease physical symptoms of anxiety can encourage your teen to be less afraid of trying out challenges.

Use Self-Talk for Facing Challenging Situations

There is one more step that your teen can take to better tolerate the situations he will confront: prepare for ways to cope with his distress. Have you noticed that people who are not very socially fearful tell themselves something that will help them get through particularly challenging times? This is fairly automatic to most people. For example, a confident teen might quickly think to himself, *I just have to get through my jitters when I first start to talk; then it will be all right.* Teens who are socially anxious do the opposite; they think of a multitude of ways that something in the future will *not* work out. So it can often be helpful for teens to deliberately make what is called a *coping statement* in their mind. Ideally, a coping statement is not all positive, but takes into account real challenges and a realistic sense of outcomes. Here are a few coping statements that address fears about giving a performance:

- It is natural to be anxious, but the anxiety won't hurt me.

- This is going to feel tough, but I can get through it.

- People may notice a few of my mistakes, but they'll also notice things I do well.

If your teen is interested, she can even write out for herself a few thoughts on an index card and call it her "coping card." Most teens prefer to do this on their own, since they understand their anxiety the best. It's most helpful for your teen to review this before facing a challenging situation; however, if your teen gets stuck, she can use it even in the midst of facing fears. Before your teen engages in this process she should first try discounting her worries. However, using coping statements before facing a fear can help your teen to push herself to follow through, despite obstacles she encounters.

Eliminate Safety Behaviors

As Chapter 4 introduced, safety behaviors help an anxious person feel more comfortable and safe in anxiety-provoking situations. The problem is, these are a subtle form of avoidance, allowing one to not feel the full force of an anxious situation. When teens use safety behaviors, they never learn that they can cope *without* them, so the behaviors maintain their anxiety. They can even make one appear less socially skilled, which is what socially anxious teens fear the most! Here are some examples of safety behaviors that anxious teens often use in social situations:

- Speaking to less intimidating members of a group

- Speaking quietly or looking down to attract less attention

- Escaping to the bathroom during a school dance

- Sitting in the corner or back row of a room

- Limiting participation in group discussions

- Drinking alcohol to feel less nervous

It may take a bit of detective work and careful observation to identify a safety behavior. But you can also be straightforward by asking: "Is there something you do to try to feel less anxious or to lessen disapproval in this situation?" Teens need to learn to face their fears by gradually reducing these safety behaviors.

> By engaging in safety behaviors, your teen never learns that the situation he is confronting is not dangerous, so his fears persist.

Identify Behaviors to Target for Change

It may help to think of social anxiety as a phobia. With a phobia, people avoid the feared object—for example, avoiding heights. With social anxiety, people avoid social situations, so the goal is to gradually reduce this avoidance. Before we can do that, we must identify behaviors that need to change. You can encourage your teen to consider, *In what specific way am I directly or more subtly avoiding social situations?* For example, Tina was avoiding calling friends over, raising her hand in class, and speaking up in class debates. These would be the potential targets for behavior change.

> Encourage your teen to make a list of social situations that she avoids. Help her remember to include even small acts of avoidance and safety behaviors, such as speaking less often.

Remember that anxious teens really do want to participate in social activities, but their anxiety prevents them from doing so. Therefore, an easy way for teens to identify targets for behavior change is to write down all of the things they would like to do if they were not so anxious. This list must be unique to their specific fears. For example, Amanda, a sixteen-year-old, came up with the following list:

- Invite a friend over to the house.

- Answer a question in class.

- Ask a teacher a question after class.

- Speak up in a crowd.

- Tell something funny to a group of friends.

- Talk to someone I don't know well.

- Give a speech.

When making this list, encourage your teen to set realistic goals, such as speaking to one new friend, or inviting one friend over, instead of trying out for the lead in a musical! Once your teen has made his list, the next step is for him to rate each behavior in terms of how much anxiety it would probably cause him to engage in the behavior. If it is too hard to decide between ratings of anxiety, your teen can simply rate behaviors as low, medium, or high on a scale for anxiety.

An important note: you should not create this list for your teen or push her to do tasks that she is not ready to do, for a host of reasons. Fears are very specific to each individual, so what is anxiety provoking for one socially anxious teen may not be for another. You also might suggest your teen practice a behavior that's far more difficult for your teen than you realize. Teens need to feel in control of this process, since anxiety, in general, makes anyone feel very out of control. Taking the first step to challenge fears is the hardest part. We want teens to experience success so that they continue to face even more challenging situations.

Face Social Fears One Step at a Time

The next step is for your teen to list the social situations she has been avoiding and to rank order them in terms of how much anxiety they may trigger, from easiest to most difficult (see Chapter 4 again for a refresher on how to create a challenge ladder). Remember that for each situation, she should stay with it, despite experiencing anxiety, and try to fully eliminate her safety behaviors. She should practice each behavior frequently until it becomes doable, at which point she can go on to the next behavior. Should she realize that facing her fears is easier than she initially thought, she can even revisit the list and perhaps add a few more challenging goals.

Exposure can take time and be challenging for your teen. Here are a few tips for increasing the effectiveness of exposure practice:

- Make sure exposures are happening frequently enough to have an impact.

- If your teen thinks the exposures aren't eliminating anxiety, remind him that the goal isn't to eliminate anxiety entirely but to tolerate new situations.

- Continue to show empathy for your teen's concerns when he resists a difficult exposure, and express confidence in him to try again.

Test Out Beliefs in the Bravest Way

Up to this point we have been talking about gradually practicing those behaviors that one typically avoids due to fears. There is an additional strategy that can further enhance the gains already achieved: When a fearful thought tells us not to do something—that doing it would result in disaster—we can deliberately do the opposite of what the thought wants us to do! Remember from Chapter 2 that this is the best way to defeat anxiety in general. In the case of social anxiety, anxious thoughts are constantly telling your teen to avoid making a social faux pas. So to challenge these thoughts, your teen has to not only stop avoiding social risk, but also *deliberately* make a social mistake!

Why would deliberately doing something "wrong" be helpful? You might assume that it would expose your teen to terrible social consequences. But what socially anxious teens define as a huge mistake is often very minor and carries little to no consequences. Socially anxious teens typically are perfectionists and think that one wrong move will result in ridicule. Deliberately making a small mistake will teach them that this is not true.

Here are a few examples of what your teen might try:

- Make a slightly silly move in gym class.

- Loudly cough in public.

- Drop books in a school hallway.

- Pause for a few seconds during a conversation.

Remember Robert, whom we met at the beginning of this chapter? To confront his worst fears, Robert might deliberately do something to bring attention to himself rather than blending in, such as speaking somewhat loudly at the lunch table. Teens who test out their perfectionistic social beliefs by making mistakes or calling attention to themselves realize that it is not really such a big deal; in fact, people often barely react. This will help reduce their feeling that the spotlight is always on them. They can also see that they can tolerate small amounts of social attention or disapproval if it occurs. All of us sometimes make minor social gaffes, so your socially anxious teen can't avoid this forever. He needs to learn that he can handle it when it naturally occurs. Again, your teen can begin by making small mistakes that most people typically would not even notice and gradually work up to more daunting gaffes.

What Teens Learn by Facing Fears

What should your teen expect if she tries to gradually face her fears? If the level of challenge in the task is well chosen, she should experience some anxiety, but at a tolerable level. If she is not anxious at all, then it is too easy a task. She should also expect that if she continues to practice a difficult challenge it will become easier over time, because as she practices, she discovers new things about herself and what she is capable of doing.

Teens can learn many useful things from facing their social fears. They learn that they can tolerate a certain amount of anxious discomfort, that most often the discomfort abates with repeated practice, and that experiencing anxiety itself is not dangerous. Even if they encounter some minor disapproval along the way, they learn that it is not so bad, and they can handle it. Most significantly, they usually realize that their anxious thoughts and beliefs about the dangers of their social environment are too extreme, and often not true at all. In other words, rather than just talking back to their fears, they *show* themselves that they are not in as much danger as they thought. Here are a few ways that the teens I have worked with have expressed a change in thought and belief:

> "I avoided dances because I thought I would look ridiculous. But I finally decided to go. I guess everyone looks a bit funny dancing, not just me. It wasn't so bad."

> "I never raised my hand in class. I always thought that people were thinking I was stupid when I got an answer wrong. After I kept practicing raising my hand, I realized that no one really cares if I get it right or wrong."

> "I never wanted to talk much at the lunch table. I thought they all secretly felt that I was awkward. Then I actually started speaking up more and got noticed in a good way. I guess I am not as bad at conversation as I thought!"

Activity: What My Teen Learned

As discussed earlier, much of the power of exposure comes from the learning that accompanies it. Teens learn that what they expected to happen didn't happen or wasn't so bad. To help your teen solidify this learning, after he tackles a challenging behavior, gently ask questions such as:

- What did you learn about your fear?

- Is the situation as bad as you thought?

- Did you find out that the bad thing that you expected to happen didn't occur?

- Did you find out that it gets easier over time?

- Were you proud of yourself for doing something challenging?

The momentum that this new learning creates helps to sustain further steps to face fears.

Does My Teen Have Social Anxiety Disorder?

Social anxiety disorder is a common anxiety disorder of adolescence. Significantly for teens, the disorder typically starts in late childhood to early adolescence (around age thirteen), and without treatment it can essentially continue throughout adulthood. So it is critical to quickly identify and stop this disorder in its tracks.

Social anxiety disorder causes many problems. Naturally the biggest is its impact on social functioning. Teens with social anxiety disorder report feeling lonelier and having fewer friends than those without it. They frequently worry and can experience panic attacks. The disorder can also lead to depression and substance abuse. When socially anxious teens engage in substance abuse, typically they are trying to reduce their feelings of anxiety.

How can you know whether your teen is just going through a typical adolescent phase or has a real disorder? You need to look at two aspects of the problem: how much distress he exhibits and how much his social functioning is affected. If your teen is experiencing significant distress and impairment in daily functioning, it is more likely he has developed the disorder. In particular, the more avoidance he practices, the more likely it is that his anxiety has become a serious problem.

If your teen's level of social anxiety is stuck on high, despite your and your teen's best efforts, it is worth seeking out a professional who specializes in this area. In combination with the skills your teen has already learned in this chapter, this may be the boost that your teen needs to overcome the problem before it becomes more entrenched.

What Does Success Look Like?

By using the techniques discussed in this chapter, socially anxious teens can make huge strides in decreasing their distress and avoidance. Again, social anxiety stops teens from doing what they really want to do. When teens make real progress, the positive changes can be remarkable! Teens will begin to take meaningful social risks, such as introducing themselves to someone new or speaking up in class, with gratifying results. They will develop a more lighthearted view of their own behavior, accepting that they make mistakes like everyone else and that no one is perfect. Lastly, they will realize that the spotlight is not always on them, so they will tend to act more freely and be more relaxed and open to new experiences. As one relieved teen whom I helped to take social risks told me, "Everyone at school is finally getting to know the real me."

6 My Perfectionistic Teen

Confronting Perfectionism and Procrastination

Sara's Story: One Step Away from Disaster

Sara, a high-achieving senior, prides herself on always "doing her best." On top of excelling in school, she plays violin in the orchestra and spends long hours editing the school newspaper. To everyone, she seems so sure of herself; however, unbeknownst to others, Sara is in the grip of anxiety. She constantly worries that she will disappoint her teachers, her parents, and most of all herself. These worries drive her to relentlessly strive for perfection.

This week was especially difficult. On Monday, she couldn't shake the worry that her teacher would think that her history essay was "disappointingly amateur," and she spent many extra hours trying to perfect it. During Wednesday's orchestra concert, even though the conductor complimented her, she felt that she had ruined her violin solo by making a small mistake. Then on Friday, despite getting an above-average grade on her English paper, she anxiously told herself, *I can't do anything right.*

Understanding Teen Perfectionism

To perfectionists like Sara, their performance is judged by only one standard—whether it is perfect or a failure. As a result, they are on a mental tightrope, hyperfocused on achieving, fearing that one wrong step will send them hurtling to their destruction. When perfectionists don't meet their absolute standards for success, they experience lots of panic that something terrible will happen. Coupled with this, they experience shame that they couldn't perform adequately and are less worthwhile because of it.

Does your teen:

- Feel that her performance is never good enough?

- Become very upset when he makes a mistake?

- Excessively review or correct her academic work?

- Procrastinate for fear of doing a less-than-perfect job?

- Discount positive aspects of his performance?

- Act anxious even when performing well?

- View criticism and mistakes in her performance as a sign of failure?

- Focus excessively on his appearance?

All of these problems are aspects of how perfectionism can manifest in teens. Adolescence brings plenty of opportunities for perfectionism to take hold. With their identity in flux, teens are primed to compare themselves to others and question whether they are competent and worthwhile. The push for academic achievement (from both parents and teens) can also unintentionally escalate perfectionism in teens. It then becomes a strategy to maintain self-worth and avoid failure.

Perfectionists continually evaluate their performance in critical ways, but in doing so they create feelings of anxiety and dread.

Is It Positive Striving or Perfectionism?

There are many teens who manage to set positive, often high goals for themselves and strive toward them without falling into unhealthy perfectionism. The question is how to differentiate between a healthy push for excellence and a damaging perfectionism.

The essential difference between positive striving and perfectionism has to do with the standards by which your teen judges competence and self-worth. The perfectionist teen sets *unrealistically high, inflexible standards* that are often impossible to attain without great personal cost. The perfectionist teen also ties self-worth to perfect behavior and complete attainment of personal goals. Since everything is tied to perfectionists' achievement, the process of achieving becomes inherently stressful, so they tend not to enjoy themselves even while achieving their goals. Instead, they live in a constant state of anxiety.

Positive strivers set realistic goals that are achievable without too great a cost to them. And unlike the perfectionist, they enjoy, rather than fear, setting challenging goals for themselves. When positive strivers make a mistake, they see it as a way to figure out how to change their behavior or modify the goal, not as a blow to their self-esteem. A positive striver, by not obsessively worrying about failure, also recovers more easily from a disappointing performance.

The Perfectionist...	Whereas Positive Strivers...
Has unrealistic goals and standards for personal performance	Set standards for excellence that are high but achievable
Cannot tolerate a less-than-perfect performance	Enjoy challenging themselves regardless of the outcome
Dwells on failure as a sign of inadequacy	Are resilient to failure and disappointment
Views making mistakes as unacceptable	Use mistakes as opportunities for growth and learning
Holds rigid rules and beliefs about how to behave	Change their level of effort depending on the importance of the task

Perfectionism ultimately is the engine that fuels anxiety and worry, whereas positive striving drives healthy achievement and joy. The next activity will help you practice differentiating between the two.

Activity: Positive Striving vs. Perfectionism

For each statement, decide whether it is an example of positive striving or perfectionism.

1. I must achieve excellence at all times.

2. I set high standards for myself and feel good when I achieve them.

3. I enjoy pushing myself to do better and learn from my mistakes.

4. If my work on a project isn't exceptional, I worry that everyone will be really disappointed in me.

5. I get upset with myself when I don't ace a test.

6. When I notice an error in my work, I feel angry with myself.

7. I feel happy when I achieve something I didn't think I could.

8. I focus a lot on whether I am meeting the standards I set for myself.

Statements 2, 3, and 7 are examples of positive striving. Notice the clear pattern here. Positive strivers set realistic standards and enjoy not only the outcome, but also the process of achieving. They see mistakes as opportunities for growth. They can still maintain high standards but are not weighed down by constant doubt and fear of making mistakes.

Perfectionism's Pitfalls

We all know the perceived "upside" to perfectionism. Teens figure that if they do everything perfectly—get perfect grades, show great talent and perfect behavior—they will avoid failure, feel especially worthwhile, and achieve social prestige as well. Yet there are huge downsides to perfectionism, many of which are not immediately obvious. As you read through this section, keep in mind how your teen's perfectionism shows itself, which will help you to identify areas for potential intervention.

Disrupted Task Performance

Anxious teens often don't realize the extent to which perfectionism can get in the way of task performance rather than help it. Most significantly, their inability to accept limitations and move on can cause major problems with task completion. For example, one teen would continually revise his essay all the way up to the deadline. He was giving this task 130 percent when he could have reserved his energies for other tasks.

Perfectionism causes an array of other academic troubles. Perfectionistic teens lose focus on the task at hand when they constantly worry about how well they are doing. Their tendency to overwork leads to fatigue and sleep deprivation, which impairs the learning process. Procrastination and indecision have their roots in perfectionism, as avoidance of making risky choices seems to be a good way to decrease anxiety. Perfectionists also tend to see their mistakes not as opportunities for growth but as threats, which impedes learning and motivation.

It is a myth that perfectionism always helps achievement. It tends to hurt task performance when one expends too much effort, avoids, procrastinates, and views mistakes as a threat.

Heightened Test Anxiety

Imagine that you thought that each question on a test represented something very important about you: not just whether you knew the answer, but so much more—whether you were smart or competent—indeed, whether you were going to succeed in life. This is the world of the teen perfectionist as she sits and takes a test. Perfectionists maintain almost impossible-to-meet standards for how they do on tests, and they fear that not meeting such standards will invariably lead to disaster.

This overemphasis on performance naturally triggers anxiety. The perfectionist tends to experience heightened dread before taking tests and then may experience concentration problems and acute anxiety, even all-out panic symptoms during the test. It is not surprising, then, that perfectionism tends to backfire, sometimes making performance worse.

Identity Concerns

The effort by teens and young adults to appear to be completely composed on the outside while hiding all of their anxiety and internal struggles has been termed the "duck syndrome." Picture a duck appearing to glide effortlessly across the water while at the same time *paddling like crazy underneath!* This is a telling metaphor for the perfectionistic teen who strives to appear cool and collected, despite being highly stressed. The term was originally coined at Stanford University, but this type of behavior is rampant at both high schools and college campuses. Appearing fine to their peers and teachers, and often even to their parents, these teens are usually model students and high achievers who hide their stress and anxiety very well.

Perfectionists feel it is a sign of weakness to show their struggles to the world. However, the costs of maintaining this façade are huge. The effort can prevent a teen who fears failure from taking risks and trying something new. Most importantly, for stress to be dealt with, it has to be acknowledged and worked on, not disguised. Such masking of anxiety can worsen loneliness, increase depression, and trigger further anxiety. These teens feel that they alone are having problems coping.

Increased Emotional Distress

Unchecked perfectionism causes many other problems. It is linked with chronic worry, performance anxiety, and social anxiety. In the latter case, perfectionists think others have the same high standards as they do for themselves and so are constantly judging them. Because perfectionists always blame themselves for anything that goes wrong, their perfectionism weakens their resilience to stress—their ability to bounce back from hardships. It plays havoc with one's self-esteem when one considers all faults and weaknesses intolerable. Feelings of worthlessness commonly arise, which can cause depression or make it worse. Excessive perfectionism about appearance can even lead to problems with body image and increase risk for eating disorders.

Activity: How Does Perfectionism Get in the Way?

The following exercise is not a laboratory test and won't tell you for sure if your teen is perfectionistic. However, the more items checked, the more you need to be on the lookout for how perfectionism might get in the way of your teen's life.

My teen...

- ☐ Often sets unrealistic goals and standards.

- ☐ Becomes very upset when minor mistakes are made.

- ☐ Only seems satisfied with perfection.

- ☐ Gets very upset when an important goal isn't reached.

- ☐ Seems too focused on avoiding any failure.

- ☐ Can't tolerate criticism well.

- ☐ Tries to create a perfect impression for others.

- ☐ Is self-critical even when achieving.

- ☐ Doesn't bounce back easily from a poor performance.

- ☐ Seems tense and worried even when doing well.

- ☐ Frequently procrastinates and is indecisive.

☐   Works to the point of exhaustion to do really well.

☐   Checks work excessively.

☐   Panics before or during tests for fear of failure.

☐   Won't try something new for fear of failing.

What do you notice about your teen's perfectionism? How does it get in the way?

Try asking yourself the same questions to determine whether perfectionism gets in the way for you as well. Knowing how we all can fall into perfectionistic behaviors at times will help you to empathize with your teen's perfectionism.

The Faulty Thinking of Perfectionism

Perfectionists tend to engage in frequent faulty thinking (see Appendix B for a list of common thinking errors). Indeed, *the hallmark of perfectionism is all-or-nothing thinking*—a tendency to see things in extreme black-and-white terms. Perfectionistic teens judge all of their behavior on whether it was a complete success or not.

Perfectionists often dismiss positive facts about the way they are achieving—the cognitive error of disqualifying the positive. Instead they focus exclusively on one negative result, no matter how small—the error of mental filter. They wrongly conclude that other people are always judging their performance negatively and are very disappointed with them—the error of mind reading. Lastly, they catastrophize by fearing that imperfection will result in intolerable disaster.

Remember Sara, the senior having a very bad week? Sara's thinking demonstrated key cognitive errors. First, she imagined that the teacher would be disappointed with her for not submitting a flawless essay—an example of mind reading. Then, by overfocusing on a mistake during her violin performance, she demonstrated the error of mental filter. At the same time, she too easily dismissed positive information that she was doing well, such as when the conductor complimented her—an example of disqualifying the positive. Lastly, by judging herself to be incompetent, she demonstrated all-or-nothing thinking. Altogether, by falling into this type of faulty thinking, she was unable to realistically evaluate her performance and accurately perceive how others might view her as well.

Changing Perfectionistic Thoughts

When parents see the impact of perfectionism on their teen, it is hard not to step in and tell him to just let it go. However, if you tell your perfectionistic teen to not get worked up about something—that what he is getting upset about isn't that important—he will most certainly discount what you have to say. To him, it feels like you are ignoring his urgent concerns. The best way to help your teen be less perfectionistic is not to tell your teen to be less perfectionistic, but to encourage him to evaluate his thoughts, either on his own or with a little gentle nudge from you.

Your teen should treat her perfectionistic thoughts like most worries—as something to be evaluated and then replaced with more realistic thoughts. For example, if Sara were asked, "In what way can you see the situation as less than a complete failure?" she might tell herself, *I guess I had a lot to juggle and did pretty well on everything. Maybe it was not so bad.* If she asked herself, *Am I overlooking ways that I am performing competently?* she might realize, *Well, my grade on my essay was above average, and my conductor complimented me on my performance.* Although it may seem obvious that Sara should notice the positives in her performance, perfectionists like Sara tend to have blinders on, focusing on only the ways that they fell short. So questions like these are helpful to spur Sara to view her situation more accurately.

Change Perfectionistic Beliefs

Once your teen can talk back to his everyday perfectionistic thoughts, the next step is to help him overcome long-standing beliefs that maintain his perfectionism.

Imagine that you told yourself, *I have to do well at everything in order to be a worthwhile human being.* Of course you can see the risk to self-esteem of having this view. Yet perfectionistic teens typically hold this underlying, extreme standard of performance. They maintain rigid rules to judge themselves and assume that others judge them by the same rules. Perfectionists need to learn that despite their mistakes, they are still acceptable, worthwhile people.

Encourage your teen to develop a more flexible self-view. You can start out by educating your teen about what is an appropriate and healthy standard for judging one's worth. For example, the next time your teen thinks she has failed, you can say, "All of us fail to achieve our goals at times, yet that doesn't diminish our successes or who we are. What are some ways that you can still feel good about yourself?" You can also encourage a broader understanding of success in your interactions with her. Ask general but challenging questions about successful people to help counter false ideas. For example, you can ask, "Is it true that successful people never make mistakes?" Or "If a successful person made a mistake, would that make them unsuccessful?" Or "Is it possible that your performance was worthwhile, even great, even if some people didn't like it?" It might be helpful to bring up famous inventors who saw each failure as an opportunity to learn. For example, consider this quote, attributed to Thomas Edison: "I have not failed. I have just found ten thousand ways that won't work." Healthier beliefs about herself and the world will gradually but powerfully translate into less perfectionism and anxiety for your teen.

Listen carefully to your teen. When he repeatedly sets goals for his performance with phrases such as "I must always," "I should," or "I have to," he could be demonstrating rigid, perfectionistic beliefs.

Reduce Perfectionism During Task Completion

Perfectionism affects all aspects of task performance, from setting goals to worrying about meeting them and finally to evaluating them critically. Usually parents have a front row seat on how perfectionism can lead to fatigue, trigger panic, and, in the worst case, result in paralysis in completing tasks. Here are some ways to help reduce perfectionistic thinking at each stage of this process.

Setting Future Goals

Perfectionists often set completely unrealistic goals, which invariably increases their risk that they will fail to meet them. If you suspect that your teen has set an unrealistic goal, you can gently question whether her goals have a good chance of being accomplished. One way to figure this out is for her to rate, on a scale of 1 to 100 percent, how likely it is that she will meet her goal in time for a deadline. If the rating is not at least 75 percent, then she might need to revise the goal. You can also ask her whether her goal is helping motivate her to do the work or getting in the way of it. Too many perfectionistic teens set goals so high that the task seems undoable, which reduces motivation. Encourage your teen to set goals that are both challenging and achievable.

Working Toward a Goal

Once perfectionists set a goal, often they will still see it as impossible to achieve. In general, they tend to underestimate their abilities and overfocus on their weaknesses. They also dread failure and frequently catastrophize about everything going wrong. To help decrease how daunting the goal feels, you can ask, "Even though this task is challenging, what are some ways that it is still doable and going well?" If your teen is catastrophizing, you can reduce a sense of doom by asking, "Even if you are having some trouble with your work, how can it still turn out okay?" The goal of such questioning is to decrease your teen's extreme perfectionistic thinking and refocus him toward productive behavior.

Reviewing Past Performance

When a performance is over, perfectionists constantly judge it with unnecessarily high standards that provoke continued anxiety. They magnify the importance of their mistakes and minimize successes. On top of that already large burden, they greatly fear that they have disappointed those whom they are trying to please. The questions that follow are all designed to overcome the black-and-white thinking and catastrophizing that perfectionists use to judge their performance. Note that asking *all* of these questions would seem too overwhelming for your teen, so choose just a few to help your teen more realistically assess the results of her work:

- Is there a way to judge your performance as not all bad, but also positive?
- How would a friend view your performance?
- How could the result not be so "make or break" for you?
- Are you magnifying the criticism and minimizing the approval?
- Could people be not as disappointed with you as you fear?

By stepping back and evaluating her thoughts in this way, your teen will better be able to proceed through challenging situations without getting caught up in acute anxiety and panic.

Experiment with Decreased Perfectionism

Changing one's thoughts and beliefs is a critical part of reducing perfectionism, but it is driven not just by how your teen thinks, but also by how your teen behaves. Perfectionistic teens are very reluctant to change their behavior, fearing that behaving this way is not a choice but a necessity. They fear that if they let go even the slightest bit, the world will discover how inadequate they are. Crucially, they have not tested whether it is necessary to be that perfectionistic. Instead, they pay more attention to outcomes that seem to confirm their beliefs. Here are some ways to modify perfectionistic beliefs by modifying behavior.

Perform Mini-Experiments

One good way to challenge perfectionism is through hypothesis testing. The idea is that perfectionists have a *wrong hypothesis* or belief about what will happen if they change their behavior. Your teen can test out how true his predictions are by doing mini-experiments. For example, if your teen feels that he has to revise an essay five times or else it will be worthless, he can instead revise it four times and notice how this impacts his grade. If your teen worries that saying something incorrectly will result in ridicule, he can deliberately make a small blunder and see that nothing terrible happens.

Of course, we don't plan experiments that are likely to backfire or cause a lot of anxiety! We reduce perfectionism just a bit and see the result. This makes it easier to tolerate. We caution teens that there might be a slight reduction in performance or a small negative result, but this is preferable to the cost of overdoing the effort or avoiding the chance of making a mistake.

Most often teens who have successfully done these experiments discovered that they had more freedom than they realized to modify their behavior. They learn that their rigid perfectionistic beliefs about how to behave are not true, and that perfectionism, far from keeping order and control in their life, often has actually made their situation worse. That can be a beautiful insight for a teen who never questioned her way of coping before.

Practice Nonperfectionistic Behaviors

The best way to encourage nonperfectionistic behaviors is with the use of exposure and response prevention strategies, as discussed in

Chapter 4. To put exposure into practice here means to deliberately do something less "perfect" and tolerate the anxiety involved. Deliberately coloring outside of the lines might be an exposure task for a perfectionistic kindergartner over-concerned with neatness! Exposure tasks for perfectionistic teens are naturally more complex but follow the same principles of doing something that's the opposite of what the perfectionism tells them to do. Your teen should begin with easy challenges and work his way up to more difficult ones.

To identify a target for exposure, consider how your teen changes her behavior in response to her perfectionistic thoughts. Usually a perfectionistic behavior is similar to things we all do (such as checking to see whether something is right), but it is done too frequently or intensely. Some perfectionists make excessive lists in an effort to never make a mistake. Gradually decreasing list making would then be a useful exposure task to repeatedly practice until it feels less anxiety provoking. If your daughter drastically overdoes the time she works on her hair and makeup in the morning, she can practice getting through it quicker. If your son continually rechecks to make sure there are no errors in his work, he can reduce the number of times that he checks.

It is important to get teens to repeatedly practice not just decreasing the way something is made perfect, but actually making small but deliberate mistakes. Breaking perfectionistic rules *on purpose* will teach your teen that there is less need for perfectionism than she thought. For example, Marie would sometimes rewrite all of her work over and over until each letter looked perfect. The handwriting looked beautiful and impossibly neat, but at too great a cost to her—she was actually unable to finish tests in class. To overcome the problem, she deliberately practiced writing in a more rapid, sloppy fashion. Her efficiency in completing tests then dramatically increased, while her anxiety gradually decreased, as she got used to this new way of behaving.

Consider as well whether your teen has been completely avoiding confronting a situation (such as auditioning for a school play) or avoiding learning a new skill due to his perfectionism. If so, encourage him to face his fear and notice that behaving imperfectly is not as terrible as he imagined.

Experimenting with nonperfectionistic behavior will teach your teen that the feared consequences are either not so likely or not so bad as she fears.

Overcoming Indecision and Procrastination

Perfectionism can sometimes lead to indecision and procrastination, both forms of avoidance. Through indecision, the perfectionist tries to avoid getting the decision wrong. The procrastinator, by avoiding beginning work, tries to avoid the risk of poor performance or failure. The avoidance of making choices and beginning work serves to greatly decrease anxiety (at least temporarily), which makes these behaviors very challenging to overcome. Here are some ideas for overcoming indecision and procrastination.

Practice Making a Decision

If your teen is showing a great deal of indecisiveness, first try to enter into some empathetic dialogue with her. After all, it is hard for all of us to make decisions. Empathize with the fear of making a mistake and help her to consider that a less-than-perfect choice may not be as catastrophic as she fears.

The next step is for your teen to practice changing her behavior. Making a decision will feel risky and can seem like jumping from one side of a small chasm to another—but regardless of the risk your teen feels, she has to steady herself and jump. Anxious teens need encouragement to see that either choice will feel strange, due to their feelings of uncertainty, so they can't wait for the choice to feel exactly "right." There are very few "perfect" decisions in life that don't feel at all nerve-wracking! Once the decision is made, your teen must try to not look back and regret it, but move forward, on to the next choice.

An indecisive teen needs ongoing practice in tolerating uncertainty and making uncomfortable decisions (starting with less important ones) in order to make progress in this area. Most often, if possible, it is best to reduce the number of choices that an indecisive teen has to face. Otherwise your teen could easily get overwhelmed with this challenge. Once in a while, if your teen is genuinely stuck on making a decision, you can ask permission to make it for him, while encouraging your teen to continue to practice making difficult choices.

Challenge "I'll Do It Later" Thoughts

To overcome procrastination, it is important to change thinking from thoughts that generate procrastination to thoughts that defeat it. When you see your teen stuck in procrastination, without being too intrusive you can offer up a few key questions. First, you can use questions to elicit specific thoughts that are driving worry. For example, if you notice that your teen appears anxious, you can say, "Is there a worry that is making it hard for you to start your work?" Since worries are typically about the future, you can bring your teen back to the present by asking "What might be something achievable, even if it is very small, that you can do today?" To decrease how intimidating the task feels, you can ask, "What are some ways that the task is doable?" Lastly, to highlight the dangers of procrastination, you can ask, "What are some downsides to waiting longer to do your work?" With a bit of practice, your teen can also try to make a habit of challenging his own thoughts about procrastinating.

The motto, originally from the philosopher Voltaire, that I share with teens is that "Perfect is the enemy of the good," since good keeps us moving along with our plan, and good can be the engine that transforms into better and better as we go along.

In order to begin making choices and taking action, perfectionists must learn to tolerate uncertainty about whether their decisions are right.

A Step-by-Step Plan to Reduce Procrastination

Perfectionists, due to their high standards, often create plans that are unrealistic, too grandiose, and too time-consuming. The problem is that the too-elaborate plan has a higher risk of failing. As Sheryl Sandberg says in her book *Lean In: Women, Work, and the Will to Lead,* "Done is better than perfect" (129). Guide your teen to create a realistic plan for success. Here are some ways to do so:

1. Break down the task into steps. This will help your teen see each step as doable and provide the structure to evaluate whether she is on track.

2. Estimate time for tasks. Before work is begun, your teen should estimate how long each step in a task will take, and then allow some additional time for underestimating how long each task will take (a common problem for perfectionists). Encourage him to follow these estimates as much as possible, which will require him to accept some limitations on his effort.

3. Identify the most important parts of a task and prioritize them. Some perfectionists get so bogged down in the little details and less essential parts of a task that they run out of time for doing what is most important.

4. Establish mini-deadlines. Earlier deadlines are useful, since they create a sense of urgency, push teens to make hard choices, and prevent them from overreaching.

5. Establish structure for when and where a task will get completed. Your teen should identify a time and place where she works best and set up a regular schedule to help minimize avoidance. It is easier to avoid something when there is no expectation for behavior.

6. Encourage attention to process versus outcome. Perfectionists tend to overfocus on the final outcome (such as getting a good grade), so much so that they under-focus on the process of

completing the task. Encourage your teen to notice what is enjoyable about the work that he is doing and to pay attention to these pleasures.

7. Notice areas of progress. Perfectionists tend to notice only things that have gone wrong. The goal here is to notice all of the positive work, including what has already been completed, not just what is left to do.

8. Build in rewards along the way. The hardest part of completing a task is starting, so rewarding initial effort can be a great motivator. Then build in small rewards for effort over time. Your teen can choose small but creative ones, like a trip out for coffee or frozen yogurt. Finally, plan a larger reward for task completion.

Lead the Way to a Healthier Mind-Set

Parents have much to offer in helping their teen shift to a healthier, less perfectionistic mind-set. Most teens do care what their parents think, and, whether they would like to admit it or not, they look to their parents to set an example for how to achieve in the world. Here are some ideas to consider.

Model Positive Striving and Normalize Imperfection

One powerful way to teach your teen about the right way to approach a task is to lead by example. Demonstrate through your everyday actions how you set realistic goals, create realistic plans, and know your limitations. You might talk in front of your teen about how you choose to let go of some things despite your ability to work on them even more. If something goes wrong, normalize mistakes and failures by making nonperfectionistic and noncatastrophic judgments about your efforts. For example, you can say, "Gee, this dish for the party didn't work out perfectly, but it still tastes great, and nothing terrible will happen if I leave it as it is." Focusing not just on outcomes but also on the enjoyment of the task will also minimize a one-dimensional view of success. Behaving in this way essentially provides your teen with a model of healthy striving and resilience.

> Demonstrate how you talk back to your own perfectionistic thoughts when they try to take hold.

Convey Your Own Standards for Success

As Chapter 1 discusses, teens are very much still in development, going through brain change and figuring out their identity. They are a wonderful work in progress and won't fully develop until their twenties. Many societal pressures, however, push teens to act as fully formed beings and reach great heights of achievement. But you can choose to make your own family standards.

Convey to your teen that making mistakes does not define him. Let him know he has time to improve and doesn't need to be perfect at everything he does. Then (and this is the hard part) back up your words with positive reinforcement when your teen displays great effort, or curiosity about learning, but has a less-than-perfect outcome. Express confidence in his abilities and notice out loud the ways that he did something well. This sends a message that the outcome, while desirable, is not the key to success or failure in life.

Support Your Teen's Positive Striving

Some parents fear that if they back off, their teen will slack off! However, parents can support positive striving, which naturally leads to success without all of the anxiety and distress involved in perfectionistic striving. Parents convey values through *what they attend to and what they encourage*. Notice and positively acknowledge your teen's behavior when she sets realistic goals, is passionate about learning, and displays the right level of effort and commitment for the task (not too much and not too little). Encourage her to view mistakes as opportunities for growth and learning, and to set future standards that are high but achievable. Lastly, encourage her to not speed down the track at one hundred miles an hour trying to be perfect at everything that she does. She should pace herself and, like any positive striver, adjust her level of effort depending upon the importance of the task. Positive strivers enjoy challenging themselves, so if your teen doesn't find anything at all fun anymore, that is a warning sign for a potential problem.

Rein in Your Own Anxious Perfectionism

Teens who grow up in a perfectionistic environment, where unrealistically high expectations are set, can develop a type of performance anxiety whereby they chronically fear disappointing others. Given all of the pressure to compete these days, do you sometimes fall into being perfectionistic about your teen's behavior? Unfortunately, worry can lead parents to catastrophize about their teens and, in the worst case, express those fears to them. For example, if the next time a teen gets a fine but less-than-perfect grade, a parent says, "You'll never get into the best college if your grades are like this!" the teen can unwittingly internalize such anxious thoughts, which can worsen the teen's own perfectionism. If you express such fears in a stressful moment, try later to discuss the more realistic thoughts, expectations, and confidence that you have in your teen. It is also important over time to make sure that you are challenging your own thinking errors, which we all fall into at times, in order to realistically assess your teen's behavior.

Signs of a New Mind-Set

High achievers, not perfectionists, typically do not feel anxious most of the time. So high anxiety is a sign that parents should intervene and help reduce the importance of perfectionism. Ultimately, you know that your teen has successfully reduced his perfectionism when he has fundamentally *changed his relationship with success and failure*. When your teen can tolerate making minor mistakes, learn from the occasional "failure," and continue to enjoy new challenges, then his anxiety will naturally diminish. Teens need time to develop this healthier mind-set, but the earlier they start, the more the teen years become an opportunity for growth.

7 My Irritable, Stressed-Out Teen

Managing Irritability, Stress, and Anxious Meltdowns

Ben's Story: Anxious with a Short Fuse

Ben, an anxious eighth-grader, was trying to hold it together, but things kept going wrong. Exhausted from staying up late the night before, he snapped at his family over breakfast. Later, in social studies, when his group struggled to complete their project, he thought, *This is a disaster. Nothing is working.* At an after-school soccer game, when his coach came down on him hard for a few bad plays, he thought, *Great. Now I am going to be benched!*

In the evening, after completing a paper at the last minute, he finally came downstairs to watch television. However, when his sister interrupted his "chill-out" time, he shouted, *"Get out of my face!"* which made his mother ground him from going out. This was the last straw. He raced to his room, slammed the door, and thought, *No one understands.*

The Anxious-Irritable Link

Your teen's anxiety and stress can sometimes bring out the worst in her, because the experience of anxiety is very burdensome to your teen. All of the "What ifs" that go through an anxious teen's mind and the constant perceptions of threat are exhausting.

Anxious irritability is a sign of an *imbalance*—that is, your teen's internal resources for managing a problem are inadequate for the demands placed upon her. When your teen was a toddler, she would likely express this failure to cope in the moment by throwing a tantrum. Fast-forward to adolescence. Teens now are faced with more complex challenges, which tax their coping ability and require greater self-control, such as when a teen who greatly fears embarrassment must calmly give a presentation in front of her class, in order to not get a poor grade. Many teens work hard to hold it together during the school day, which often results in anxious, irritable behavior spilling out at home. Here are some typical examples of how anxiety might present as irritable behavior in a teen:

- "Mom, you didn't wash my shirt. Now I am going to look stupid because nothing matches!"

- "Rachel interrupted me when I was working on my project, and now it is ruined!"

- "Why did you make me late? I might as well not go. Now everyone will look at me weird!"

If your teen becomes very overwhelmed, his irritability can even emerge in nonverbal ways—he might glare at you, slam a door, or kick something.

Along with irritability, restlessness, muscle tension, distractibility, and sleep problems can all be a consequence of anxiety's far-reaching effects.

Is My Teen Just Moody?

As every parent of a teen knows, the transition to adolescence can be tumultuous. Suddenly you observe mood swings, extra focus on appearance, concerns about social standing, and academic worries on a scale never experienced before. The biological changes teens are going through make them naturally moody. Their sleep problems add up over time. And they tend to hide the impact of stress and anxiety on them until it comes bursting out. In this context, it is hard to know what is moody, typical teenage behavior and what is true anxious-irritable behavior.

When psychologists assess for a problem, we typically look at the *frequency, severity, and duration* of a behavior. Most of us can be irritable and anxious at times, which is a normal aspect of dealing with everyday stress and pressure. And when we are feeling irritable, it is usual for any of us to become more easily frustrated and less flexible. However, teens experiencing chronic anxiety and irritability will express it more frequently and for longer periods of time than they will with everyday moodiness. And their irritability will be more severe than typical grumpiness. Here are a few signs to help differentiate between the two:

Signs of Normal Teenage Irritability

- Demonstrates periodic frustration with daily stressors

- Has occasional moodiness but maintains a sense of humor

- Sometimes dislikes talking to parents and siblings and wants to be alone

- Occasionally is sarcastic or snaps at requests

- Is more irritable at times of high stress and later calms down

- Appears content and joyful on many occasions

Signs of Anxious Irritability

- Appears upset over the smallest of things

- Acts irritable for frequent and long periods of time

- Is easily overwhelmed during social interactions and often withdraws into isolation

- Frequently snaps at others

- Appears tense and nervous

Is My Teen Depressed?

Another common cause of irritable behavior is depressed mood, which can range from mildly irritable or low mood all the way to full-blown severe depression. Learning about the signs of depression will help you to determine when irritability in your anxious teen might be partly depression-based and, if so, to take steps to alleviate the depression. Here are some things to watch out for:

Signs of Depression

- Is irritable or has a low mood for lengthy periods of time

- Feels sad and hopeless about the future

- Loses interest in and motivation for previously enjoyable activities

- Has a change in sleep, appetite, weight, or energy

- Withdraws from social interactions

- Has feelings of worthlessness and, in the worst case, thoughts about dying

- Has reduced functioning across home, school, and extracurricular activities

Anxiety and depression share many symptoms and manifestations. In addition to irritability, both can cause sleeplessness, fatigue, poor concentration, and reduced school performance. Teens can be both anxious and depressed, which can especially worsen irritable behavior. Note that the incidence of depression increases greatly during puberty, and depressed adolescents sometimes display only an irritable mood, not a sad one. Given the overlap between depression and anxiety, don't hesitate to seek professional help to sort through the particular causes of irritable behavior and poor coping.

The Impact of Poor Coping

Before we move on to learning how to decrease irritability in your anxious teen, it is important to first stop and consider the impact of this problem. Next to avoidance, this is one of the main ways that anxiety can significantly affect family life. Parents of anxious teens are often on edge, wondering when their teen will next snap at them or fall into a stressed-out mood. Faced with a difficult situation, a parent might modify household rules or change routines in an effort to prevent irritable behavior from occurring. Sometimes parents tiptoe around their teen, trying to avoid the next outburst. However, when they do this their teen never learns positive coping strategies, and the extra support needed to manage irritability often leaves parents feeling frustrated and resentful.

> For some teens, anxiety manifests only as irritability and is often misperceived as teen moodiness or defiance.

Reducing Irritable Behavior in an Anxious Teen

Despite the challenges involved, parents have much to offer to their anxious, irritable teens. Teens are often so caught up in their daily activities and increasing levels of stress that they don't realize how their behavior and mood are changing. Soon enough, though, the combination of poor coping, increased anxiety, and irritability begins to have a destructive effect. Here are some ways that parents can intervene to reduce this behavior or even stop it altogether.

Identify Triggers That Lead to Anxiety and Irritability

It is helpful to consider irritable behavior in an anxious teen as the *endpoint* in a sequence of events. First come the triggers of anxiety and stress. Next comes the teen's perception of those triggers as threatening, and finally comes the behavior itself. Unfortunately, many parents consider only the irritable behavior itself and not the cause. For example, one parent said, "During the ski trip, she was so irritable all weekend long and then made the ride home terrible for all of us with her poor attitude. I don't know what is wrong with her." It turns out that their daughter had been anxious about her performance while skiing, perceived the day to be very challenging, and exhibited her worst level of irritability when she was especially tired. So in order to understand anxious, irritable behavior, we have to understand the context in which it arises.

It is helpful to begin with some detective work to figure out what might be triggering your teen's feelings of anxiety and difficulty coping. First look for patterns across behaviors and situations that point to important triggers. Tracking episodes of anxiety and irritability over time will help you determine whether a particular pattern emerges. Initially, start with common triggers that would make anyone feel grumpy. Being hungry, tired, and excessively busy can impact any teen. Not having enough downtime can be a common culprit of teen irritability, along with sleep deprivation. Once you consider common triggers, consider your child's unique triggers of irritability. Ask yourself, *What situations does my teen encounter that seem to cause or worsen an anxious or irritable mood?* Here are some additional questions to consider:

- When did my teen first begin to show anxiety or difficulty coping?

- What triggers occurred earlier in the day or days before that might have caused a change in mood?

- Was there a trigger that seemed particularly meaningful and challenging?

- How did my teen perceive these triggers?

If your teen looks upset, you can ask, "What is bothering you about this situation?" Pay close attention to how your teen perceives the triggers and whether those triggers tend to reoccur. Considering all of these questions will help you better understand the way your teen uniquely responds to stress with anxiety and irritability.

Activity: Noticing What Makes Things Worse

For the next week, keep in mind the preceding questions and watch for triggers that are connected to increased irritability. You may choose to keep track of those triggers in a journal. Particularly notice whether certain triggers occur reliably over time. Then consider how your teen seemed to perceive these triggers. What did you notice? With this information, begin to consider whether it might be possible to modify any of those triggers to decrease anxiety and irritability.

Head Off the Problem Early On

Once you have identified key triggers that lead to anxiety, it is useful to try to change those triggers in order to lessen your teen's irritability. This concept of intervening early on to modify behavior is based on the behaviorist ABC model of learning. The "A" in the ABC model stands for *antecedent*—what occurs before the behavior. The "B" stands for the *behavior* itself, and "C" stands for *consequence*—what occurs after the behavior. We can use this model to intervene with anxious, stressed-out, and irritable behavior. Specifically, while we often overfocus on consequences (what happens after a behavior occurs) as a means to control behavior, this model reminds us that behavior is also impacted by antecedent events—what occurs before the behavior. In essence, to help modify the behavior, we must be proactive, figuring out ways to intervene as early as possible *before* the irritable behavior occurs.

In his book *The Explosive Child*, psychologist Ross Greene makes the point that when parents try to respond to difficult behavior, they typically intervene with the application of consequences—an ineffective approach with some kids. He recommends instead modifying the early triggers that lead to difficult behavior. Intervening before a behavior occurs can be even more important than intervening afterward, because it may prevent the negative behavior from occurring at all.

When you intervene to reduce triggers of stress and anxiety, make sure that you are not allowing your teen to avoid things that she should be learning to cope with. As discussed in Chapter 4, when we allow teens to repeatedly avoid facing anxious situations, their avoidance serves only to worsen their anxiety. Your teen needs to gradually face anxiety-provoking situations, despite her fear. So be careful to focus on modifying triggers of stress and anxiety that are not related to chronic avoidance.

For example, consider Jasmine, who worries excessively about her performance during her soccer games and wants to skip the next one. She has a sleepover scheduled the night before and an essay due the next day. In this case, her parents need to encourage her to attend the game, rather than skip it, so as not to reward her avoidance. However, they also postpone the sleepover to the next day, since the additional tiredness and time pressure to get her essay done is likely to make her anxiety worse.

Matthew is a thirteen-year-old who every night worries about someone breaking into the house. His worries were significantly heightened after he watched a horror movie with his friends. Since his parents discovered this trigger of his anxiety, they are limiting the types of movies that he sees until his worries have decreased.

Regarding Ben, the anxious eighth-grader whom we met at the beginning of the chapter, we can proactively think of many ways to help. Intervening early on might first require addressing his sleep problems. Without enough sleep, Ben is sure to be irritable. We also might help him problem solve how to handle the ups and downs of doing a group project in social studies. This might help him to catastrophize less and be more assertive with his partners. He might also need to work on his time-management skills, since his completing a paper at the last minute naturally adds to his anxiety and stress. Ultimately, by intervening on the different pathways that produce stress and anxiety, we can reduce anxious and irritable behavior.

Now consider ways that you might intervene early on to interrupt the path from trigger to anxious perceptions to irritable behavior.

> Ask yourself, *How can I proactively intervene to reduce unnecessary triggers of stress and anxiety?*

Shine a Light on the Problem

For your teen to change his behavior, he first needs to know what he needs to change and why it is important to change. Therefore, when you notice your teen beginning to spiral into increased irritability, you need to shine a light on the problem. First, describe the behavior you are concerned about and inquire about what might be bothering him. Give your teen time to respond, and provide empathy. Then, once you have empathized with your teen, clearly label the behavior that you would like him to change. You can emphasize the need to learn new ways of coping and remind him of your support.

For example, you can say to your teen, "Lately you seem to get easily upset, and you've begun to snap when we try to ask you a question. What is bothering you to make you behave this way? It sounds like you've had a really hard week, but I want you to practice snapping less when you are asked a question. It could be helpful to work on some ways to reduce some of the pressure you are under. I am always willing to help."

Often parents are so busy dealing with each episode of irritability that they never get to the root of the problem. With this new approach, you accomplish a number of things: you empathize with the problem that your teen is experiencing, begin a dialogue as to what factors might be causing the irritability, and set a limit for disrespectful behavior, making it clear that it needs to be reduced.

It is often hard to set limits with teens when they are so obviously overwhelmed and upset. Parents sometimes get used to outbursts and inappropriate behaviors; however, by letting this behavior go, they reinforce it and make it more likely to occur the next time. When the behavior crosses a line (such as screaming, cursing, hitting, throwing things), warn your teen in advance of a concrete consequence (such as a loss of a privilege), and follow through consistently. Empathize with the feelings of distress that led to the problem, but make sure to set a limit. This will encourage your teen to practice positive coping skills. To do otherwise would be to enable misbehavior due to the anxiety, which sets a bad precedent.

Encourage Self-Monitoring

A surprisingly powerful intervention in and of itself is to monitor our behavior over time. Studies show that by simply doing that, we can decrease how often a problematic behavior occurs. Imagine if you were pushed to monitor how many times you demonstrated poor posture over the day. By just paying more attention to it, you might naturally straighten up your shoulders.

Your teen can self-monitor in a quick and easy way by having her rate the level of her daily anxiety or irritability on a scale of 1 to 10. She can ask herself, *What is the rating for today, and how high did it get this past week?* Your teen might also consider, *What made it worse and what made it better?* After using this monitoring system, a teen said to me, "Well, it shot up to a 7 today because I was worried about the test I had to take, but it was a 4 yesterday. This week I noticed that it went down after I had some time to relax, and it shot up when I was rushing to meet a deadline." The more your teen gets into the habit of becoming aware of her moods and what triggers a change in them, the more she will be able to control this over time. Note that if the average level of anxiety stays high on a regular basis, your teen is at risk for her anxiety to escalate to a severe level on a very stressful day.

To really get to the bottom of what is stressing your teen, it can be helpful for him to self-monitor with a stress log. For any major triggers of stress, he can briefly record the following:

My Stress Log

- **Trigger of Stress:** What event or situation stressed me out?

- **Thought:** How did I perceive the situation that led me to feel stressed? *List some thoughts that you had about the situation.*

- **Feeling:** How anxious or stressed-out did I feel? *Rate from 1 (least) to 10 (most).*

- **Behavior:** What did I do when I was stressed?

- **What Helped?** What worked to reduce my stress and anxiety?

- **What Else Can I Think?** Change thoughts if they are unrealistic.

- **What Else Can I Do?** Change coping behaviors if they are not working.

A downloadable worksheet is available at http://www.newharbin ger.com/34657. (See the back of the book for more information.) If your teen completes a log like this, it will reveal whether thoughts are unrealistic and whether coping strategies are ineffective. If this is the case, the log encourages a change in thinking to more realistic thoughts and a change in coping to better strategies. Then, over time your teen can use it to figure out what works to relieve stress and anxiety.

Do not try to force your teen to complete the log; this tends to defeat the purpose. Instead, make sure the control stays with your teen. An empathetic talk about the benefits of checking in with your-self in this way is a more effective way to encourage participation.

Attend to Positive Coping

Teens and their parents often get into full-scale arguments over a teen's frustrating behavior. However, this can inadvertently give attention to negative coping and increase the frequency of negative behavior. It can also especially prolong conflicts, since it takes two to tango—arguing is so much easier when there is someone to argue with!

The best thing to do when your teen expresses irritability is to *purposely control your reaction*. Behave in a calm, neutral manner and try to ignore the negative behavior as much as possible. For example, if there is mild argumentativeness, ignore it. Redirect only when necessary. No matter how difficult your teen's behavior is, notice small moments of success, and pay particular attention to times when your teen copes positively in the face of an anxiety-provoking or stressful situation. As mentioned in Chapter 2, attention itself serves as a natural reinforcer and can increase positive (as well as negative) behavior over time. Thus attending to even small instances of positive behavior can have a powerful positive impact.

> Focus your attention on times that your teen displays positive coping and less irritability, even if his behavior isn't perfect.

Decrease Environmental Stress

When your teen is experiencing stress, there are only two choices for managing it: either change the nature of the stress itself or change your perception of it. There is no "one size fits all" approach for managing environmental stress. Each teen's ability to tolerate stress is different and even varies depending on the teen's stage of development and life circumstances. The more skills your teen has in her toolkit for managing stress and anxiety, the better. Maintaining good problem-solving skills is a significant step toward improved coping. Another important strategy involves facing fears and decreasing avoidance, which will reduce anxiety over time.

Parents may have to decide that something has to give—and to completely remove a source of pressure and stress. For example, one teen was otherwise happy and functioned well until a second sport was added to her weekly commitments. Her parents soon realized that, without any downtime, she had no time to decompress, and her irritability and anxiety were too easily triggered. Once the second sport was dropped (with their teen's agreement and understanding), their daughter returned to her typical self. This is a hard call for parents and teens to make; however, it can deliver great benefits in stress reduction and a calmer, more functional teen.

Decrease Subjective Stress

When environmental stress can't be modified, the goal is to decrease your teen's subjective sense of stress—that is, how your teen perceives stressful situations. Teens need help to see that the stress they are experiencing, although challenging, is less dangerous than they think. Socratic questions to decrease worry are a good strategy to use in this situation (see Appendix A for a list of Socratic questions). These questions can serve to minimize the significance of stress. For example, if your teen is worked up thinking that he has an impossible task to undertake, you can ask, "Could this situation be more doable than you think it is?" If your teen has kept a stress log to monitor the triggers of his stress, he can, with your help, use the log information to talk back to his anxious thoughts about stressful situations.

For those teens reticent to volunteer information about how they are doing, a useful strategy to try is the *weekly chat*. With older teens, I have called this a *coffee break*. It is a time specifically reserved for positive communication and support. During this chat, you can gently inquire as to what was stressful during the past week, how your teen handled it, and what is concerning about the coming week. To make it especially effective, try to engage in active listening, which means to restate in your own words what you have heard your teen say, and use Socratic questioning to reduce subjective stress. For example, you can ask "What are some ways that the upcoming situation may not turn out as bad as you think?" Then provide empathy for what your teen is going through and problem solve with him to reduce future stress. Engaging in positive communication about stress in this way can counteract its harmful effects over time.

Here is an example in which the weekly chat made an enormous difference. Jake was rapidly losing weight, to the concern of his pediatrician and the bewilderment of his family. As it turned out, Jake would easily get anxious about his schoolwork, tended to isolate himself in his room, and was reluctant to share information with his parents. So usually when he left his room his father would immediately corner him and ask blunt questions, such as "Have you been wasting time procrastinating again?" Jake began to increasingly dread leaving his room and would even skip meals to avoid getting accosted with questions. To solve this problem, I recommended a weekly or if necessary twice-weekly chat in which his parents could ask for and receive information. In return, his family agreed not to question him every chance they got. In these chats, his parents actually helped Jake to problem solve through a few challenging situations. Jake gained the weight back, and, equally important, he and his family gained a new positive way of communicating.

Model Adaptive Ways of Handling Stress

At one point or another in our lives, all of us have had this experience: matters that stress us out seem insurmountable, and we quickly become anxious and irritable. Along with asking your teen to self-monitor, try monitoring for a week or two how you yourself perceive and deal with stress. Armed with the knowledge of how your own internal world works, ask yourself, *Which ways of thinking and behaving help me to feel less anxious and stressed, and which make things worse?* Then begin to practice and demonstrate a new way of coping.

You can first show how you reduce the significance of a difficult situation by changing how you perceive it. For example, the next time you notice that your anxious thoughts exaggerated a threat, you can say something out loud, like "I worry that things are going to go completely wrong, but I know that these are just my worries talking to me.

Things are not so bad." Then, during a stressful moment, make an effort to show your teen how you practice positive ways of dealing with stress. You can also share with her how you coped with an especially difficult situation, which helps to normalize the effort to deal with stress and pressure. Put a sudden change of plans into perspective to demonstrate how you deal with unpredictability. Lastly, show how you take a time-out to relax when needed, ask for support, or decrease your workload. Over time, by modeling adaptive methods of coping with stress, you *show* rather than tell your teen how to think and behave in a productive fashion to reduce anxiety, stress, and irritability.

> By showing how you deal with stress and pressure with positive coping and stress-reduction activities, you serve as a model for your teen to build her own coping skills.

Help Your Teen Tolerate Change

Anxious teens tend to demonstrate less overall flexibility in the way that they cope with situations. They may rigidly expect routines to stay the same, resist the smallest change in a schedule, or avoid trying something new. If they are forced to go outside of their limited comfort zone, they often react with fear, irritability, and anger. This pattern of behavior is backed up by research on anxious children, which suggests that children with high anxiety show an *increased need for control and predictability* in their lives. Typically, when that control is threatened by something suddenly changing, irritable behavior emerges.

Since anxious teens never do well with chaotic situations, parents can help to increase a general sense of predictability by creating consistent rules and expectations at home. Advance warnings of changes to any plan are also useful. Obviously, this is not always possible, and your teen can't be shielded from all of life's unexpected problems. Providing too much protection here would reduce his resilience to change.

But you can gradually encourage your teen to learn to tolerate the everyday uncertainty in the world and move toward coping with small changes. Empathize with the desire for things to stay the same, and at the same time push for gradual exposure to change. Deliberate exposure practice can also be used to help your teen in this area (see Chapter 4 for information about setting up a challenge ladder). For example, your teen can work on getting used to a sudden change in routine. Balancing out a certain level of predictability with opportunities to tolerate unpredictability will help your teen better manage the unpredictable life stressors that he will confront.

Enhance Family Coping

Any plan to address irritability and stress can't neglect the impact of family functioning on teens. General stress and anxiety management are supported or hampered by the overall atmosphere at home. For example, a teen's developing problems with coping are likely to catch everyone off guard if family members don't communicate well. Also, teens with anxiety rarely do well when there are unpredictable household rules, frequent family discord, or too chaotic an environment. Here are some ideas for reducing stress, enhancing communication, and maintaining a positive household structure for your teen:

- Establish rules and routines that ensure a fair level of predictability.

- Each parent should consistently apply the same rules and routines as the other.

- Allow frequent opportunities for positive communication that is not centered around stressful topics such as grades, chores, or household rules.

- When you all need to discuss a high-conflict topic, set up a time to talk with your teen rather than communicating at unpredictable or stressful times.

- Establish small moments of bonding between parents and children with a focus on empathy and positive attention.

- Strive to give siblings equal amounts of attention over time.

- Recognize and respect that in the teen years children need an increased level of privacy and independence.

- Each person in the house (don't forget yourself in this!) needs rest and downtime to recharge and reduce irritability.

Notice that across many of these varied suggestions, the key dimension to work on is *communication*. Communication with your teen should be clear, consistent, and predictable and focused on positive behaviors, not just negative. No matter how your teen behaves, providing warmth and support will increase her resilience to stress. Continue to offer love and support, no matter whether your teen acts irritable or angry. Over time, a warm family atmosphere is like a safety net. It encourages your teen to take reasonable risks and face new challenges—and catches your teen if she falls.

Activity: Our Household Stress Meter

Pause and examine your own family's functioning to determine whether changes might be necessary. If there was a meter to rate how much household stress your family has, what might it show? Despite the hectic pace everyone follows, take this opportunity to stop and think about the impact of stress on your family. Ask yourself the following questions:

- ☐ Is there enough consistency and structure in rules and routines to create predictability?

- ☐ Do members of the household snap at each other due to the stress they are under?

- ☐ Are people in the family overburdened by too much on their plate?

- ☐ Are there enough opportunities for each family member to have downtime?

☐   Are there enough opportunities for respectful and planned communication among family members?

☐   Are there opportunities for positive interactions among family members?

☐   Do parents communicate with each other about effective ways to coparent?

☐   Are there marital issues that need to be focused on?

☐   Does my teen have opportunities for some independence and control?

Many of us rarely stop to think about our individual or family functioning until irritability and anxiety suddenly flare up. Now that you have had an opportunity to examine your household's stress level, consider whether changes are necessary. If you noticed an area that needs some work, identify three ideas for a proactive family stress plan to address the problem. Then put the plan into place.

Managing Anxious Meltdowns

Up to this point we have been discussing how to reduce episodes of irritability in your anxious teen. Now we'll turn to the even greater challenge parents face: when their teen has a major meltdown. Many anxious teens at some point experience a "straw that broke the camel's back" moment. Suddenly having to face a severe trigger of anxiety and feeling unprepared to cope with it, they experience full-on panic. Then there is all-out distress and acute anxiety. This is often accompanied by tearfulness, anger, frustration, and defiance, as teens' fighting instincts are brought to the fore during a crisis. This is essentially the "fight" in the fight-or-flight response, when your teen feels like he is facing imminent danger head-on. Dealing with meltdowns can be an exhausting experience for both parents and teens.

To understand the anatomy of a meltdown, it is important to look at what teens are thinking, feeling, and doing at this time. Their thoughts are typically very irrational and often involve catastrophic fears that the worst has happened or is about to happen. As one teen told me, "When I thought that I was going to fail my test, all I was thinking was...*Aah, I'm going to die. I'm going to die.*" That describes the teen brain on emergency overdrive! When teens become extremely anxious, they often feel physical symptoms of panic in their body and act as if they are under threat. While their behaviors might seem illogical and irrational, they feel driven to act that way, given the emergency they feel is upon them.

> Major symptoms of panic include shortness of breath, rapid heartbeat, sweating, nausea, trembling, and dizziness.

When your teen is in the midst of a crisis, what *doesn't* work is to try to intervene with advice or problem solving. Since his emotions are intensified and his thoughts are irrational, he can't begin to process this information. The advice also agitates him more because it becomes just another thing to try to cope with. Some teens, rather than resist interaction, try to pick a fight and relentlessly press their parents for attention. This defiant behavior can serve as a form of avoidance, allowing teens to avoid, in the moment, facing their feeling of being overwhelmed.

Parents' own fight-or-flight response can be activated when their teen is having a meltdown and screaming or behaving aggressively. This is a critical time, because if parents respond angrily or try to strongly discipline the teen, the meltdown can escalate. So parents must work very hard to stay calm in the midst of the storm. The goal essentially is to maintain safety and to let the meltdown subside. Here are effective ways to respond during a meltdown:

- Model a state of quiet attentive calm and acknowledge feelings of distress.

  Example: "You are feeling really upset right now."

- Don't engage; instead, step back and resist being drawn into an argument.

  Example: "We'll talk soon."

- Let your teen know that her distress will pass in time.

  Example: "After a while, you will feel less upset."

- If your teen is acting not only anxious but also aggressive, redirect him to stop his aggressive behavior and go to a quiet place to get calm. Separate yourself from your teen too.

  Example: "You need to stop this behavior; go to your room and stay there until you feel more calm. I am going to be taking a time-out for myself as well."

- Let the meltdown subside before trying to give advice.

  Example: "I'll help you with the problem soon."

After the Meltdown

Once your teen is again calm and back to thinking more clearly (which may take some hours or even a day), regroup to consider what happened. Ask your teen in a neutral, supportive manner what she thought happened to cause the meltdown and how things might go differently next time. Did she notice particular thoughts that were getting out of control? Was something said that particularly bothered her (perhaps questions asked of her at a time of high anxiety)? Did she notice that she felt increasingly more stressed or a situation felt too challenging? If she can identify specific triggers that led to the meltdown, it will help to prevent future escalations. If the meltdown led to behavior that crossed the line, such as hitting, insulting, or destroying property, your teen should either make amends the next day in some productive way or receive a consequence.

Teens, like adults, have different levels of insight about their own internal world. If your teen doesn't notice any problems, this tells you how in tune he is—or isn't—with his own stress and anxiety levels. If that is the case, you should check in with your teen earlier in the cycle to jog him to notice changes in his mood and behavior. For example, if your teen has had several sleepless nights and then begins acting very irritably, ask him whether he is noticing the effect of poor sleep. When you and your teen better understand what is going on earlier in the cycle, you can develop a proactive plan to address the problem.

Parents, not just teens, may need a time-out after a meltdown before they can feel calm enough to again work on problem solving with their teen.

Back to Problem Solving

Once the dust has settled, and your teen is calmer and thinking more logically, it is time to see whether problem solving is necessary. The trigger of a meltdown does not have to be related to the crux of the problem. In fact, sometimes it can be many steps away from it! For example, a teen who is essentially worried about whether he will pass a test might get upset if his house was too noisy for focused study. Importantly though, a teen's perceptions that a problem is unsolvable often drive anxious behavior. So you need to find out whether there is a problem to be solved and what it might be. Here are some issues to discuss with your teen:

- What went wrong?

- Is there really a problem to be solved, or could faulty thinking be triggering anxiety or making it worse?

- If there is a problem, what are some ideas to fix the situation?

- If the situation can't be fixed, what are some ways to cope with it?

When It Works

You know your approach is working when your teen demonstrates less irritability over time and appears better able to cope with the anxiety and stress in her life. Importantly, a natural consequence of improved coping with anxiety and stress is increased resilience to stress. Resilience to stress means that your teen is more likely to bounce back from difficult experiences. For anxious teens, becoming resilient to stress helps increase their confidence over time for taking reasonable risks in new situations, rather than avoiding stressors. Overall, parents have an enormous influence in helping their anxious teen become more resilient. When you make an investment in both your teen's health and your overall family's health, the rewards are truly great.

8 Quieting the Body's Alarm System

Reducing Panic, Decreasing Physical Symptoms, and Calming the Mind

Lily's Story: Panicking About Panic

After Lily left health class, where the teacher had discussed fainting, she became worried that she might faint sometime. The thought frightened her, as she imagined everyone looking down on her collapsed body with amusement. Lily quickly began to feel dizzy, hot, and not herself. As she walked down the hallway to her next class, she felt her legs go numb and began to tremble a little. The worse she felt, the more she panicked about how she was feeling; soon she began struggling to breathe. Seated in her next class, she couldn't help but think that something terrible was happening to her. *I need to leave class right now or else I will faint*, she thought.

Misperceiving Anxiety's Alarm

What all anxious teens have in common, no matter how their anxiety manifests, is a *biologically based alarm system* that can go off unexpectedly when a threat seems near. This alarm system causes physical sensations—most of them highly uncomfortable—ranging from the mildest stomachache, caused by a slight feeling of danger, to a full-blown panic attack, which can happen when danger feels acute.

Teens' biggest misperception when these physical sensations arise is that they are caused by something other than anxiety! Once they have a misperception like this, it can cause all kinds of trouble, because teens start acting like their misperceptions are true. For example, if a teen thinks the physical sensations mean that he is really ill, he may seek medical intervention or avoid activities or situations because of his "illness."

Even if teens know that their physical distress is due to anxiety, they tend to misperceive the physical sensations as dangerous in some way, which further triggers the body's alarms. For example, an anxious teen who is experiencing nausea due to anxiety may think this means that she is going to throw up, which makes her more anxious. Or a teen struggling through a panic attack may think that her dizziness and panic symptoms are dangerous signs that she will faint, go "crazy," or embarrass herself in front of others. This chapter focuses on applying strategies to reverse this process—by correcting the misperceptions and changing the behavior.

Dealing with the Physical Signs of Anxiety

To help teens manage and reduce their physical symptoms of anxiety, we need a multipronged approach. We will apply key strategies, which you have previously learned, such as modifying thinking and reducing avoidance, along with some new ones to quiet the body's alarm system. It starts with your teen's perceiving the physical sensations that accompany anxiety as harmless and then calming the body to decrease those sensations. Then, by engaging in repeated exposure to situations that feel dangerous, your teen learns that nothing bad happens when she confronts these situations. Concurrently, your teen should engage in strategies that minimize the importance of the sensations, such as challenging negative thoughts about them. Let's take a look at this approach.

Immediately Label Discomfort as "Anxiety Talking"

Just as "beauty is in the eye of the beholder," the way we think of our physical state is entirely subjective and dependent upon our circumstances. If you run a mile, you naturally notice your racing heart, sweaty palms, and rapid breathing as a sign of health, not danger. Yet if you got those same symptoms when resting, you would probably become very concerned. Doctors' offices, and even emergency rooms, handle visits from frightened people who mistakenly perceive a panic attack as a sign of a serious problem. With the help of parents, teens can learn that they are not in danger and instead correctly interpret what is happening to them in the moment. The following two dialogues suggest how to help teens quickly relabel their physical sensations as harmless and not a sign of illness or danger:

Teen: I don't want to go to school today. I feel sick again. I think I might throw up.

Parent: You've been feeling pretty anxious the past couple of days. Anxiety can especially make our stomach feel upset and trick us into thinking we are ill. Remind yourself that this is just anxiety bothering you, and you can handle school today.

Teen   *(calling from school):* When I was taking my test, I got so anxious—then I couldn't breathe, and my legs felt numb. Come pick me up. I think something is really wrong.

Parent: That must have felt really bad and scary. When we are very anxious, our bodies sometimes overreact to it. You are okay. This is anxiety causing a false alarm. Rest for a while, but then try to return to class when your body calms down.

It takes practice for teens to recognize their physical sensations as just anxiety talking and not something to get worked up about. But the more they get into the habit of labeling their physical distress as a harmless consequence of anxiety itself, the more this will prevent anxiety from escalating, both in the moment and over time.

Help Your Teen Understand the Body's Alarm System

Once your teen gets the immediate message that he is not in danger, he needs to learn more about what is really happening to him.

Most teens don't even realize that anxiety has a profound effect on the body and can be accompanied by a cascade of uncomfortable physical sensations. Without this understanding, their frightened response sets off worsening anxiety and further exacerbates the physical sensations. High anxiety can cause a multitude of changes in the body, such as:

- Rapid breathing

- Shortness of breath

- Feelings of choking, tightness in the throat, or difficulty swallowing

- Dizziness or light-headedness

- Rapid or very noticeable heartbeat

- Chest pain or discomfort

- Sweating

- Feeling hot or cold

- Trembling or shaking

- Numbness or tingling sensations (especially in the hands or feet)

- Nausea, abdominal discomfort, or stomachache

You don't need to list all of these symptoms for your teen, but do educate her about the relevant ones that she has experienced. Remind your teen that while anxiety "speaks loudly" sometimes, these symptoms, each on their own or in combination, are not harmful, although they may feel frightening. Let your teen know that the sooner she recognizes and labels these symptoms as anxiety when they occur, the easier it will be to feel less afraid.

Many teens with high anxiety will struggle with the new experience of having a panic attack. If your teen experiences a surge in fear or discomfort that rises to a peak within minutes, along with most or all of the physical symptoms just listed, he is likely experiencing a panic attack. Panic attacks can be expected, meaning a situation arises that is known to trigger them, or unexpected—coming out of the blue. Most first panic attacks happen during a period of high stress, making anxious teens who are sensitive to stress all the more vulnerable.

Panic attack symptoms are basically the *faulty activation of the fight-or-flight response*. The body overreacts to the sense of danger by going into full threat-response mode, which unfortunately includes physical responses. For example, during the fight-or-flight response, heart rate and breathing speed up to bring in more blood and oxygen to the muscles to be better able to fight or flee. Digestion slows, since we don't need to digest food when under extreme threat, but this creates nausea. Other symptoms, such as light-headedness and numbness, are aftereffects of this survival response.

During a panic attack, important cognitive symptoms can occur: a feeling of unreality, of being detached from oneself; a fear of losing control or going crazy, or a fear of dying. Naturally, if you don't know what is happening to you, being hit with a panic attack (or even experiencing some of the symptoms) can be very scary and make you feel completely out of control.

If your teen is experiencing panic attacks, it is important to explain what a panic attack *is* (a sudden episode of bodily response to intense fear, which feels very uncomfortable but is not dangerous) and what it is *not* (going crazy or dying). Teach your teen that these sensations, even if severe, naturally subside within a short time. No one permanently suffers from or is harmed by a panic attack. Explain that this surge of fear is actually a normal and natural response to what's perceived as a real danger, except that it is a misfire—no actual danger exists.

Note that many teens who get panic attacks are afraid of fainting because they feel very light-headed; however, it is quite rare for a person to faint. The extreme activation of the nervous system during a panic attack is physiologically the opposite of what happens during fainting. Fainting is caused by a sudden drop in heart rate or blood pressure, whereas when we are anxious, our heart rate and blood pressure rise.

Note: If your teen has a phobia about blood, injections, or injury, the response may differ. His physiological response to this phobia can cause an initial blood pressure rise but then a sudden drop, which *can* result in light-headedness and fainting. If your teen is susceptible to this problem, seek advice from a therapist on how to address the phobia, which is very treatable. Additionally, speak to your teen's physician about a useful strategy that prevents fainting in this circumstance; called the *applied tension technique*, it involves tensing the arms and the lower legs for ten to fifteen seconds, pausing, and then repeating this a few times.

If your teen has milder but more long-lasting physical symptoms, such as fatigue, muscle tension, headache, or stomachache, he may have a more ongoing moderate level of anxiety. These symptoms are usually associated with chronic worrying and anxiety, which puts the body into a state of continual mild to moderate alert. Often teens misperceive these types of symptoms as a sign of physical illness and thus take them too seriously. Teach your anxious teen again that these symptoms are a consequence of persistent anxiety and should not be viewed as a sign of either illness or danger.

Panic attacks rarely occur in children but increase around puberty, making teens susceptible to a first attack particularly when under stress.

Reverse the Perpetual Anxiety Cycle

Remember the perpetual anxiety cycle discussed in Chapter 1? Anxiety's three elements—cognitive, physical, and behavioral—interact to trigger and worsen anxiety. Teens don't automatically realize how these parts can influence each other to maintain their physical distress. Specifically, if your teen views her physical symptoms as dangerous and then avoids situations, that can set off a vicious cycle: the beliefs about the symptom and the behavioral avoidance come together to worsen anxiety, which can worsen the physical symptom itself. For example, if your teen thinks her shortness of breath means that she can't breathe (anxious thought), this thought will cause intense anxiety, and then lead to her trying desperately to escape the situation (behavior), which leads to more anxiety and likely even more shortness of breath.

Try to engage your teen in looking at how her thoughts and behaviors are keeping anxiety going. To help your teen become more aware of the impact of how her thoughts, feelings, and behavior interact, ask, "Notice what makes the anxiety worse—a thought, a stressful situation, a physical sensation—and then notice what you do in response."

As your teen practices observing her feelings, thoughts, and behaviors, she is likely to realize how these are feeding into her anxiety and making it worse. You can also add gentle input, such as "By leaving so quickly when you felt unwell, you never got to notice that you could handle the situation. Why not try next time to stay in the situation and see how it isn't as bad as you fear?" The next exercise will further help you evaluate how the anxiety cycle is affecting your teen and where to intervene.

Activity: My Teen's Perpetual Anxiety Cycle

Ask yourself the following questions to determine how your teen's perspective on his physical signs of anxiety and his reactions to them might be contributing to his anxiety problem.

Does my teen:

☐ View his physical signs of anxiety as dangerous?

☐ Frequently get distressed about his physical signs of anxiety?

☐ Have a fear of his physical signs of anxiety that leads to avoidance?

☐ Feel that avoidance of situations keeps him safe?

☐ Repeatedly check whether he has physical signs of anxiety?

☐ Seek reassurance about his physical signs of anxiety?

Each question checked indicates an impact of physical symptoms on anxious thoughts, feelings, or behaviors. If every question or most questions are checked, this indicates that the perpetual anxiety cycle is fully in play.

Research suggests that believing panic symptoms are harmful is a risk factor for the onset of more attacks. This belief naturally leads to fear and avoidance, which leads to more panic.

Help Challenge Catastrophic Thoughts

Anxious thoughts can send catastrophic messages about what a physical symptom means; however, teens can talk back to those anxious thoughts. Here are some examples of catastrophic thoughts teens might have about their physical symptoms:

- *If I get light-headed, I will faint and everyone will look at me funny.*

- *If my heart beats that fast again, I will have a heart attack.*

- *If I throw up on the bus, people will think I am weird.*

- *If I can't catch my breath, I will die.*

You'll see that in many cases teens don't fear physical danger alone, but also a socially disastrous consequence of having physical symptoms. Many teens, due to the social sensitivity that comes with adolescence, often imagine that others will notice their physical symptoms of anxiety, exposing them to embarrassment and humiliation. If your teen is afraid of the social consequences of her symptoms, review Chapter 5 for addressing social fears. Teens need to learn to tolerate the possibility of peers noticing their symptoms and the slight chance of embarrassment. While most teens think that everyone can see how they are feeling inside, in actuality most report that when they were having a panic attack, no one around them even showed any recognition.

Although it is easier said than done, encourage your teen to challenge her negative thoughts in the moment when her body overreacts to anxiety. A teen fearful of fainting can say to herself, *I am a little dizzy, but so what? It will go away and isn't going to hurt me. My thoughts are just tricking me that I am going to faint.* Challenging thoughts in this way can even get easier over time. Sienna successfully repeated to herself a shorthand version of herself challenging thoughts: *So what?* She said this to herself any time she experienced light-headedness during the school day, which helped her to get through each period of her day. Teens who learn to discount their negative thoughts find that they feel more in control, despite physical symptoms still arising unpredictably.

Activity: Identify and Challenge Catastrophic Thoughts

It is helpful to figure out what specific catastrophic thoughts your teen is having about his physical symptoms, in advance of his facing a fearful situation. To find this out, ask him, "If you experience _____ [physical symptom, such as dizziness], what do you think will happen then, and what is the worst that could happen?" Once you are aware of these specific thoughts, encourage your teen to talk back to these thoughts. Your teen can do this by reminding himself that these sensations are harmless and that, based on what he knows, a catastrophic physical or social consequence is unlikely to happen. Make a note of these thoughts for future reference to make sure your teen is gradually challenging and eliminating them.

Model a State of Empathetic Calm

Parents have another important role to play in encouraging realistic thinking. Most anxious teens watch their parents' reactions as a way to figure out if they are in danger. If parents act worried and upset in response to their teen's physical symptoms, it sends the teen a message that her fears may be warranted. If you observe your teen in distress, it is important to stay calm; this helps send a message that there is really nothing to fear. Remind your teen that it is a false alarm, then encourage your teen to not escape, but rather stay put in the situation until her discomfort subsides. Don't forget to also empathize with what your teen is going through, since the physical symptom is real and can feel really bad! The goal is to convey, with both your words and your behavior, *Even though it feels horrible and scary, it is not an emergency. You can get through this, and it will feel better soon.*

If your teen is having a full-blown panic attack, with multiple severe symptoms, this is a sign that the fight-or-flight response has been fully activated and it may not be possible to stop it immediately. In that case, both parents and teens may just have to ride out the physical discomfort and fear until they subside (like riding out a storm). Calmly convey the message, though, that the panic attack will subside shortly.

One dilemma for parents (and for teens) is that it is sometimes hard to know if teens who feel unwell are really sick. Anxious teens, by mislabeling themselves as "sick," often persuade their parents to check as if the teen is truly ill. For example, a teen may say he is feeling hot and repeatedly ask for his temperature to be taken. However, if your teen is feeling an uncomfortable physical sensation along with high anxiety, it is a pretty safe bet that the physical symptom is anxiety-related. In this case, it is especially important for you not to react as if your teen has a medical illness.

Even if you suspect that your teen is truly physically ill, acting calm in responding to minor physical illness sends a message that there is no emergency and that your teen can deal with everyday illness as well. When in doubt, getting a consult from your teen's pediatrician about the nature of a symptom can reassure both your teen and yourself that there is no need for alarm.

Calm the Body

Especially when symptoms escalate and become very uncomfortable, it is easy to imagine that something is really wrong. The goal, therefore, is to calm down the body's overreaction to danger as quickly as possible.

The best way to counter anxiety's effects on the body is through a technique called *belly breathing*. To belly breathe means to breathe slowly and deeply. There is nothing terribly fancy about breathing this way; it is what newborns do—natural, deep breathing. The important thing is that it counteracts how people typically breathe when they feel very anxious—too rapidly and shallowly, which causes shortness of breath, light-headedness, a rapid heart rate, and other symptoms. Belly breathing helps send a message to your teen's nervous system to reduce or even stop the fight-or-flight response.

Here's a simple exercise your teen can try to learn how to belly breathe. You'll want to try it as well to know how best to coach your teen in this strategy. You can do this sitting or lying down.

1. Put one hand on your belly and one on your chest.

2. As you inhale, bring the air down into your belly and let your belly inflate outward. Notice that your hand is moving outward.

3. Exhale and let your belly naturally and smoothly deflate.

4. Make sure you are breathing at a slow steady pace (no big, sudden forcing of breath in or out).

5. If you notice the hand on your chest rising more than the hand on your belly, this is a sign that you are doing more chest breathing than belly breathing. Chest breathing is more shallow breathing. Try to make sure your chest moves less and your belly moves more. But don't really stress about it. It takes practice to learn a new way of breathing.

One good way for your teen to practice belly breathing is by lying on her bed and resting a light book on her belly. Then she can try to make the book rise up and down just through her breathing. Once your teen learns belly breathing, there is no need for her to keep putting a hand on the belly and one on the chest. She can do this type of gentle breathing anywhere and any time. Teens might be especially sensitive about being observed doing this in front of others; however, one great thing about this breathing strategy is that no one can even tell that they are doing it.

Belly breathing is useful to do when physical symptoms begin to emerge and trigger anxiety. It will help your teen feel more in control in a situation when uncomfortable sensations arise and, since it encourages slow breathing, it potentially prevents panic symptoms (such as rapid breathing and dizziness). By reducing distress, it can also prevent further avoidance. It can even become a preventative tool to relax the body every day. Relaxed breathing then becomes a simple but powerful technique to keep everyday anxiety at a minimal level, which will serve as a buffer against stress.

Reduce Avoidance and Practice Exposure

Chapters 2 and 4 describe the importance of *exposure with response prevention* as a strategy to reduce anxiety. Exposure is also very important to use as a strategy to decrease physical symptoms. Many teens avoid situations because of their fear of experiencing uncomfortable physical sensations. This type of avoidance prevents your teen's learning that these sensations are harmless and tolerable. For example, Lisa, who after having her first panic attack was fearful of getting dizzy, began to avoid any situation that might cause her to feel dizzy, including cheerleading and dance class. Once avoidance begins, it often spirals from situation to situation, leading a teen to restrict more and more activities to avoid feeling physically uncomfortable. This increasing avoidance ultimately strengthens fears and makes it more likely that physical symptoms will appear and stick around.

It is naturally very hard for parents to watch teens suffer through a full-blown panic attack or an attack of nausea. However, by trying to help teens reduce their discomfort, parents sometimes accidentally reward avoidance. When you allow your teen to avoid certain places or activities that bring on physical distress, avoidance sneaks in the backdoor and is strengthened. For example, when you pick up a teen from school immediately following a panic attack or allow your teen to stay home from dance class because of a bout of dizziness, you help reinforce the idea that perceived danger must be avoided.

To tackle avoidance head-on, first help your teen understand that avoidance feels better at first but then makes both fears and the physical symptoms of anxiety worse. Then consider all of the ways your teen is avoiding situations due to her fear of having physical symptoms and, using strategies described in Chapter 4, help your teen to make a challenge ladder. If your teen resists challenging her fears, you may need to put your coach's hat on and supportively but firmly push her to do so, while expressing confidence in her ability to get through tough times.

Once your teen is on board with a plan, help her to gradually face each situation without trying to lessen her discomfort in the moment until her anxiety decreases. That will help decrease those physical symptoms over time.

An especially counterintuitive strategy to reduce fear of physical symptoms uses repeated exposure to those physical symptoms! In this approach, teens use specific exercises to deliberately induce physical sensations that mimic those they experience when anxious. This strategy can help any time the teen fears experiencing physical symptoms, and it's especially helpful in treating panic disorder, a condition in which one has a persistent fear of getting more panic attacks. Here are some ways that the physical sensations can be brought on:

- Spin around for up to one minute to produce a mild level of dizziness.

- Run vigorously for one minute to produce a racing heart and shortness of breath.

- Breathe through a straw for one or two minutes to feel short of breath.

By doing these exercises repeatedly until anxiety decreases, teens learn to directly experience and cope with the physical sensations that they fear most. This type of exposure specifically teaches several important things:

- Physical sensations such as dizziness are part of our body's normal response, since they can be evoked through normal activities.

- Just like with any other exposure, the sensations can be tolerated and gotten used to.

- The physical sensations, even if uncomfortable, are not harmful.

Note: While these exercises are not dangerous on their own, since people run and children spin for fun, teens with certain medical conditions, such as asthma, should first have these exercises approved by their family physician.

> To reduce even partial avoidance, ask, "In what ways are you trying to keep yourself from experiencing uncomfortable physical sensations?" Encourage your teen to face those situations step by step.

Reduce Checking and Reassurance

As teens struggle to cope with the physical symptoms of anxiety, it is quite common for them to become hyperfocused on whether they are in trouble. Teens often scan their bodies for symptoms, which serves only to heighten their effect. Next they are worrying about where the problem could happen and what activities might bring it on. The purpose of all of this vigilance is to avoid any situation or activity that will make their physical symptom worse. However, all of this hyperfocus generally backfires. Rather than reducing discomfort, it increases it by giving the symptoms too much importance.

Teens often involve their parents to check on their physical symptoms and provide reassurance. A teen might say, "I feel a little dizzy right now. Do you think I am okay?" A supportive parent can sometimes get drawn in to repeatedly giving reassurance that there is nothing wrong. However, the more teens obsess over their physical symptoms and ask for reassurance, the more this can feed into their irrational thoughts of danger and make things worse. Again, there is no amount of reassurance that will fully assuage your teen's feelings of uncertainty. The goal is to help him learn to recognize the false alarm and tolerate the discomfort and anxiety.

Although it is difficult, let your teen know that you need to gradually hold back the reassurance, to help her learn to get used to the physical sensations on her own and practice not giving them so much importance. Here is an example of a parent accidentally giving in to excess checking and reassurance:

Teen: Mom, I woke up feeling weird again. Do you think I am all right?

Parent: Of course you are fine. Remember, I told you yesterday that you were okay. Nothing is wrong with you. I will check on you soon.

Here is how the same parent might avoid giving the teen excessive reassurance:

Teen: Mom, I woke up feeling weird again. Do you think I am all right?

Parent: Remember when we talked about false alarms? It is time to talk back to your fears and remind yourself that you can handle those feelings.

Parents need to also reduce the checking they themselves do. For example, if a parent knows that her teen suffers from physical symptoms due to anxiety, it is best to downplay checking. One teen was doing great until her concerned parent texted her, "Are you feeling okay?" which prompted her to check in on herself, notice her physical symptoms, and become anxious. This behavior also unintentionally reinforces the idea that a teen can't tolerate his symptoms and might need help.

Teens need to be encouraged to become *less internally focused* on their anxiety symptoms and more focused on the outside world. Some teens especially have trouble resisting a tendency to check on anxiety symptoms during downtime, when their thoughts naturally turn inward. If your teen frequently dwells on physical discomfort, encourage an outward focus (such as thinking about a pleasant upcoming activity); the less monitoring of physical symptoms of anxiety, the better. Over time, as teens practice less reassurance seeking, more acceptance of their symptoms, and less self-monitoring of symptoms, they will be less aware of troubling symptoms and find that these don't stick around as long.

> Your teen can make a note of what to say to anxiety the next time that it sends a false danger signal. Then when she has an urge to seek reassurance about a physical sensation, she can refer to the note instead.

Calm the Mind

The mind sends feedback to the body and vice versa, so strategies to calm the mind support calming both body and mind, which helps to keep anxiety as well as physical symptoms at bay. Research suggests meditation and mindfulness strategies are very effective in decreasing anxiety and calming the mind. To meditate means to quietly focus one's mind for a period of time; mindfulness means to step back and observe your thoughts, feelings, and behaviors.

Despite the mystique surrounding it, the components of good meditation are deceptively simple. It starts with concentrating on a mental image, repeating a word silently, or even just focusing on the breath as it goes in and out. The point is to have something to focus on that will help to steady the mind. Then the aim is to just stay calmly focused. When a random thought comes into the mind, gently bring the attention back to the point of conscious focus.

Meditating for as little as five to ten minutes a day can calm the mind. Any activity that promotes a concentrated focus on the present (mindfulness) can be relaxing and help your teen feel less anxious. Here are a few additional ideas for creating a sense of mindful calm:

- Coloring (in books designed for teens and adults) as well as engaging in other types of artwork can instill a calm, meditative focus and be fun as well.

- While taking a walk, your teen can mindfully notice (be completely present and aware in the here and now) the sights, sounds, and smells along the path.

- While sitting, your teen can just notice her breath without trying to change or interfere with it and, as random thoughts arise, bring a focus back to the breath.

- While listening to music, your teen can immerse himself in the sounds and notice the way he is feeling in the present moment.

- To learn meditation and mindfulness activities, your teen might prefer to download an app that helps her engage in and track her meditation/mindfulness strategies (see Appendix E for a few suggestions).

Meditation and general mindfulness strategies can be very effective in coping with and reducing anxiety. Anxious teens often find it hard to separate their anxious thoughts from themselves. Through practicing meditation and mindfulness, they learn how to *detach from thoughts* (no matter how disruptive or anxiety-provoking those thoughts are) and stay focused on the present moment. Then, when the next anxious thought tries to intrude on the mind, your teen may find it easier to bring focus back to what is important. Anxious teens, like all of us, often get caught up in worrying about and striving for the future. These strategies encourage *the opposite of striving* for something—they allow us to simply be in the present moment. For teens who are rushing to achieve, this is a way to pause and center themselves before they go on to the next challenge.

> Learning to be mindful can be the ultimate powerful way that your teen bases his behaviors on his own values and goals, and less on anxiety "talking" to him.

A New Way of Being

It is possible, with practice, for your teen to get really good at mastering anxiety and the physical discomfort that comes with it. Teens can learn to change how they think, feel, and act when discomfort arises. Anxious thoughts become just thoughts, anxious feelings become just feelings, and physical symptoms of anxiety become just harmless sensations. And with effort, teens engage in behaviors that ignore anxiety, so they don't fall into the trap that avoidance creates. With this new way of being, it just gets easier over time to resist anxiety's call.

You can really tell when positive change has occurred, when your teen seems to be more concerned with "what I really want to do right now." Kaitlyn, having faced and overcome her fears of panic, proudly said, "Sometimes my body gets worked up, but now I just go with the flow, and focus on what is really important in the moment." Zachary remarked, "Anxiety wanted me to avoid the party because I might feel sick, but I told it to get lost." Emily said, "If the panic comes, I let the storm pass by, but it doesn't stop me." Cutting through the noise of anxiety means getting back to what life is really about—friends, family, and the freedom to be in charge again, no matter what your body or anxious thoughts might have to say about it.

9 Anxiety Flashpoints Through the Teen Years

Modifying Triggers of Adolescent Anxiety and Understanding Anxiety Disorders

So far, we have emphasized modifying your teen's specific anxiety problem. However, the time has come to take a broader view and consider the ways that anxiety develops through the teen years. Step back and remember when your child was young. By learning about early childhood behavior and being told what to expect, you were able to monitor and prevent problems from worsening. Similarly, this chapter seeks to offer a window into when anxiety might emerge, so that you can proactively take steps to deal with it or even prevent it from rising.

The focus here is on what I call *"anxiety flashpoints"*—times during adolescence when many teens may experience an increase in anxiety. Some of these flashpoints are what most teens experience as typical stressors, and some involve unexpected, often negative events.

While much anxiety in the teen years comes and goes, flashpoints can sometimes trigger the beginnings of an anxiety disorder, so the latter part of the chapter will address what to do if you suspect your teen has developed an anxiety disorder. Anxiety disorders can also sometimes arise without a connection to a specific negative event. In this case, the culprit may be the expression of genes that enhance vulnerability to disorders. However, even in this circumstance, stress often worsens symptoms of anxiety. So, no matter the origin of anxiety, it is helpful to develop a broad-based plan to reduce stress in the teen years.

Managing Anxiety Flashpoints

Anxiety frequently emerges when one of two things happens: *increased uncertainty about the future* or *increased stress*. Typically the uncertainty leads to lots of "What ifs" that keep the engine of anxiety going, while stressful challenges make your teen doubt her ability to cope. Due to their identity being in flux, teenagers can quickly lose all perspective when a negative event occurs. In this section we look at some key ways that changes during the teen years combine with both uncertainty and stress to trigger feelings of anxiety. As you read through these flashpoints, imagine how your own teen might react to each and how you could begin to intervene. Regardless of what issue your teen is struggling with, the first and most important intervention is to provide empathy and validation for the struggles she is coping with. By putting yourself in your teen's shoes, you will show your teen that you are ready to understand what she is going through and ready to help.

Adjusting to Middle School

Many preteens and teens find the transition to middle school anxiety-provoking. Usually, the complexity of middle school seems daunting, with its larger facility, multiple teachers and classrooms, and need for students to be more organized. Aside from those basic concerns, during this stage of development, teens worry about whether they will fit in or something they do might make them appear different. Taken together, those worries heighten the stress of adjusting to their new situation.

In August, Rebecca began to intensely worry about the start of middle school. She imagined that she would lose her way in school and then be embarrassingly late to class. She thought she would be the only one who couldn't get her locker open; she imagined the bus leaving without her. She liked her old school, which felt small, safe, and familiar. Now she figured that the homework was going to be really difficult and that she would not be able to cope.

If your preteen is worried about middle school like Rebecca, here are some tips for dealing with this transition:

- Whenever possible, let your preteen tour his new school, try out his new locker (or learn how to work a combination lock) and orient himself to his new surroundings.

- Normalize the feeling of being in a whirlwind of change as something that every preteen feels is disorienting but will subside as your preteen gets used to it. Tell her that she will feel more in control soon.

- Encourage your preteen to identify and use the supports around him (teachers, guidance counselors, friends), to help him problem solve.

- Remind your preteen of other situations that seemed daunting at first but now seem routine (like going away to camp or learning a new sport), and express confidence that she will get used to the change.

- To boost a student's organizational skills, encourage your teen to stop and evaluate whether his system for organization is working (from the start of being assigned a task to turning it in) and, if necessary, create a new system. Your teen should consider, *Where in the process is the system falling down?* (for example, forgetting to turn completed homework in) and *What strategy will fix it?* (for example, having a separate homework folder).

Coping with a Change in Peer Group

Teens rely on their peers to bolster their identity and guide them through the ups and downs of adolescence. So when there is a sudden shift in that group, a teen can become very anxious. And these shifts in peer groups are quite common in adolescence. Teens who were friends in elementary school can become less close as they grow older and develop new interests. Sometimes, because of social pressures, a teen will even suddenly decide to completely ignore a good friend. Cliques begin to form around common interests or common ways of behaving. Within this changing social scene, teens feel pressure to join the "right" group, and some try to drastically modify their behavior in order to fit in. In the midst of this pressure, a teen who is excluded from a peer group or overtly bullied can feel especially anxious and vulnerable.

At the start of middle school, David noticed that his good friend Will was beginning to pay him less attention. Will had gotten more into sports and was now hanging around with friends from his travel soccer team. Soccer wasn't David's thing. He had tried to hang out with Will's group but felt that he didn't fit in there. This led to a lot of anxiety until he decided to switch lunch tables. Now he was getting to know new friends who shared his interest in robotics.

If your teen is coping with a change in peer group like David, here are some tips for managing this flashpoint:

- Encourage your teen to be proactive in making new friends by seeking out opportunities to meet new people and taking risks to introduce herself to others. If your teen is fearful about taking social risks, see Chapter 5 for ways to reduce social fears.

- Provide guidance, but don't direct your teen to join a particular group, which usually backfires, as teens prefer to make independent decisions in this area.

- Normalize this change as something that happens to many people. If you went through this as a teen, it may be helpful to share the experience, as long as it is discussed as an opportunity for growth, not fear.

- While peers will naturally remain important to your teen, encourage activities that broaden his identity and interests beyond fitting into one particular peer group. Also encourage diversity in his relationships across his activities. This will allow him to avoid putting all of his eggs in one basket, should he have a problem with one particular group.

- If you suspect that your teen is being bullied, empathize and provide a sounding board for your teen to develop and practice strategies for responding. If necessary, and especially if the bullying persists, seek support for your teen (whether through beginning therapy for your teen, communicating with your teen's school, or both).

Starting High School

Many students perceive the transition to high school as daunting. They fearfully realize that now grades *count*. Some become concerned about meeting their future goals and begin to imagine lots of "What ifs." For example, a teen might wonder, *What if I can't handle the extra homework or I bomb a class?* Despite having had success in middle school, anxious students rarely think about their positive coping abilities and experience in dealing with these pressures. To them, it feels like they are entering a whole new world.

Abby's panic attacks began when she started high school. Abby had become increasingly anxious and spent a great deal of time, in class and out, worrying that she couldn't cope with the change. High school seemed so much more challenging than middle school. When she didn't understand a question in class, she thought, *Everyone else seems to know this except me.* When she studied for her first big test, she thought, *This test is going to really affect my GPA and my future.*

If, like Abby, your teen is fearful of the transition to high school, here are some tips for managing this flashpoint:

- If your teen has not yet begun high school, remind her that things always seem more burdensome when we anticipate future problems, but when we get to face them head on, they are often not as bad as we fear.

- If your teen has just started high school, encourage him to notice things that have gone well, not just things that have gone wrong. If you catch your teen expressing a "What if" question about the future, encourage a realistic focus on the present.

- Remind your teen to consider all of the ways that she already knows how to succeed in high school, such as knowing how to study, organize, and learn complex material.

- Support opportunities for your teen to maintain and grow friendships, which will serve as a buffer against the stress that he experiences.

- To help diminish anxiety about not meeting parental expectations, set up expectations at home for good effort and not for perfect outcomes.

> Despite success in middle school, anxious students rarely think about their positive coping abilities and experience when they face dealing with high school pressures. To them, it feels like they are entering a whole new world.

Dealing with a Relationship Loss

Adolescence frequently involves dealing with a significant relationship loss, something many teens must cope with for the first time. Losing a close friendship or losing a boyfriend or girlfriend can shake a teen's identity, which often is already very tenuous during these years. Many teens feel worthless and catastrophize about what this means for their future.

Joseph felt shocked. His girlfriend had just broken up with him, and he imagined it was because he had done something stupid. Plus, she was always the really outgoing one at school, so now he thought that he would be ignored. In addition to sadness, he felt a terrible uncertainty.

If, like Joseph, your teen has experienced a relationship loss, here are some ways you as a parent can help:

- A strong bond with parents will help teens withstand the ups and downs in their outside relationships. Make opportunities for sharing by offering structured family times, such as sit-down meals and weekly chats.

- If your teen is catastrophizing about what this relationship loss means for her, steer her toward noticing and challenging her unrealistic thoughts.

- Encourage continued growth in identity through individual pursuits that promote confidence.

- Suggest activities that promote self-soothing (unique to your teen's particular interests), to help provide distraction and relaxation.

- Encourage your teen to have varied interests, activities, and relationships. This will help him be less dependent and less overly focused on one relationship to the exclusion of all else.

Experiencing Family Conflict and Divorce

Family conflict and divorce hit all children hard, but teens have their own particular burden to face. They are often keenly aware of and absorb family conflict more than young children do. And being on the brink of adulthood, teens are more easily pulled into the middle of the conflict. They may serve to mediate communication between parents and can feel pressured to support one parent over the other. If divorce happens, the teen likely will have to adjust to living in two homes with two different routines. Teens already have so much on their plate, in terms of academic and social demands, that this additional stress can be the final straw.

Everything changed when Kate's parents decided to divorce. She moved away from her friends, and her dad moved to another home. Now her parents often communicated with each other through her or sometimes argued right in front of her. She tried to keep the peace, but the burden felt nerve-wracking, and she feared making the conflict worse. If only things could go back to the way they were before.

If, like Kate, your teen has gone through a difficult time of family conflict and divorce, here are some ways to help:

- Empathize with the difficulty of coping with numerous changes, emphasize the enduring family bonds, and establish predictable routines. This will help your teen experience a sense of understanding, safety, and security, despite the changes going on in the family.

- Give your teen permission to not choose sides, and help her to have a healthy relationship with each parent.

- Encourage your teen to not overfocus on family conflict to the exclusion of his own independence and growth.

- Establish consistent rules and positive, clear communication with your teen and between the parents.

- Especially make sure your teen is not caught in the middle, serving as a go-between for communication between parents; settle your differences in private, away from your teen.

Coping with the Illness or Death of a Loved One

For teens coping with the illness of a family member, life often becomes even more unpredictable. Medical treatments can vary from month to month, and the prognosis is often uncertain. Some teens begin to chronically worry about their parents' health, which leads to more anxiety about the future.

The death of a family member (for teenagers, most often a grandparent) can feel particularly traumatic. Sometimes the loss can even worsen a preexisting level of anxiety, such as separation anxiety, and make teens fearful that another loved one will die. Given many teens' tendency to hide their feelings, the extent of their grief and anxiety about this loss may not be immediately evident.

Sandra was shocked and upset when her grandmother, with whom she was close, suddenly died. It made her worry about whether her own mother was going to become ill and die also. Her fears were worst right before bedtime, when she would imagine that her mother was ill and wasn't telling her. She began asking her mother each night for reassurance that she was well, but despite the reassurance, the fears kept returning.

If your teen, like Sandra, is experiencing anxiety surrounding illness or death, here are some ways to help:

- To support your teen in coping with illness in the family, provide information to help your teen understand the nature of the illness (including the expected ups and downs), which will help it seem more predictable.

- Celebrate even small ways that each family member bounces back from adversity and demonstrates resilience. This supports an atmosphere of positive coping.

- If a family member is very ill or dying, make sure your teen is not left in the dark about the illness. Without enough information, teens (and all children) fill in the blanks, sometimes imagining things that may not be occurring. Just as adults do, teens need time to adjust to changes and grieve. Provide a balanced level of information (not too little and not too much) depending on your teen's age.

- When a significant person dies, encourage your teen to process his feelings. If he doesn't feel like talking about it, it can help to write in a journal, express emotions through music, or write a good-bye letter.

- If your teen is having repetitive daily thoughts about a loved one getting ill (without any evidence that is the case), encourage her to label this as a "worry trick" that she should label as such and not treat as important.

Encourage teens to express feelings about a relationship loss, divorce, or loss of a loved one; this will help them process and recover from their sense of loss.

Adjusting to Significant Physical Injury or Illness

When teens themselves experience a significant physical illness, it can be severely stressful on multiple fronts. The physical symptoms interfere with day-to-day functioning, making it difficult to do schoolwork and keep up with everyday life. It can cause social isolation at times, which means they lose social support. Symptoms that vary from day to day can make life very unpredictable. And chronic illness in particular can make teens feel different from their peers, which in turn can make them feel insecure.

Sophia's concussion caused a lot of unexpected anxiety for her. She was used to feeling very confident in class and was always the one people turned to for help. Now, the concussion had affected her memory, which caused her to doubt her answers, but she resisted asking others, including her teacher, for help. As time went by and the symptoms persisted, she began to isolate herself, not letting others know how much she was struggling in her daily life. Even worse, she avoided taking on any new challenges, however small, fearing that she was completely unprepared to face them.

If your teen, like Sophia, is facing significant physical injury or illness, here are some ways to help:

- Acknowledge and empathize with how challenging everything now feels. Then encourage your teen to judge success not by how he was before, but by how he is positively coping now.

- While noticing her strengths, encourage your teen to acknowledge weaknesses, even if temporary. Avoidance of thinking about hardships will not help your teen cope with them.

- Your teen may need temporary school accommodations to decrease the burden of schoolwork during his recovery, or ongoing accommodations if he has a chronic illness.

- Experiencing illness can cause your teen to feel irritable, due to either the symptoms she suffers from or the stress she is under. (See Chapter 7 for ideas on how to manage irritable behavior.) During a flare-up of symptoms, be patient with episodes of irritability and pay attention to signs of positive coping behavior.

- Be careful not to engage in overprotection, despite the hardships your teen is going through. Gradually encourage your teen to face new challenges, as long as he is physically ready for them. In other words, don't let anxiety lead the way.

- Both injury and illness can knock us off our game—whether it be sports, academics, or both—leading to a loss of competitive status. The next section, about facing competition, offers ways to help teens cope with this loss.

Facing Greater Competition

During the teenage years, your teen faces many new, highly competitive experiences. For the first time ever, your teen might be taking a crucial final exam, trying out for a competitive team, or competing in an important tournament. Across all of these areas, teens now feel that they are expected to be smarter, faster, or stronger than their peers. Naturally, this can induce performance anxiety and lead to catastrophizing that they will not meet these expectations. Teens often imagine that a single negative outcome, or a few, will continue into the future (an example of the cognitive error of overgeneralizing).

Adam knew that only five spots were open for this year's debate competition team. He had been practicing nonstop to improve his performance, but with the greater pressure, he ended up not concentrating as well and making silly mistakes. He imagined that everyone noticed how badly he performed, which made his anxious feelings worse.

If, like Adam, your teen is experiencing the pressures of a competitive environment, here are some ways to help:

- Let him know that his value and worth as a person do not change despite a negative outcome.

- Signal to your teen that striving in a healthy manner to achieve goals is not the same as striving for perfection (see Chapter 6 on perfectionism for more ideas on becoming a positive striver).

- Encourage your teen to focus on the enjoyable process of achieving and passion for his work or talent so that any losses in competition do not provoke a sense of failure.

- Encourage your teen to notice thinking errors that increase a sense of danger, such as catastrophizing (fearing the worst), mind reading (imagining others are thinking negatively about you), or overgeneralizing (viewing a single negative result as an ongoing pattern of defeat). (See Chapter 3 for more ways to decrease worry.)

- Encourage a focus on individual performance goals (and passion for the activity) rather than a comparison in rankings to competitors. A marked overfocus (by teens as well as their parents) on rank may increase anxiety, decrease concentration, and likely lower performance.

- Striving to succeed without taking sufficient breaks is a recipe for exhaustion and anxiety. Encourage downtime to de-stress and let go.

Facing the Future

This broad category is for anxiety triggered by fears about the future, which most teens experience frequently on their way to adulthood. Such fears make teens question whether they have what it takes to succeed in life. Lots of things can trigger such fears—taking a standardized test such as the SAT, applying to college, knowing a sports recruiter is watching a game, or trying to get a job for the first time. Your teen's anxiety about the future will be based on two key areas of perception—how dangerous the future seems, and how confident she is that she can cope with such danger. If your teen imagines a scary and challenging future, and perceives her abilities and strengths to be limited, that will naturally trigger anxiety.

Isabella had a lot on her mind. She was set to take the SAT but felt like things were moving too fast for her. Soon she would apply to college, and she didn't even know what she wanted to do. She wondered, *What if I pick the wrong college?* and *What if I don't find a job that I like or one that I'm good at?* The closer she got to adulthood, the more she worried about what her future would be like.

If, like Isabella, your teen gets very nervous about how her future will work out, here are some ways to help:

- Build your teen's confidence in her coping ability by noticing and positively acknowledging times that she handles a difficult situation well. This will naturally decrease anxiety about the future, as your teen becomes a more confident problem solver.

- Turn worries about the future into concrete problem-solving activities. For example, help your teen break down the task of getting a job into creating a resumé, researching or canvassing the area for openings, dropping off resumés, following up, and then preparing for an interview. Engaging in concrete tasks will bring your teen's thoughts back into the present and keep his focus on things he can control.

- When your teen is stuck in the "What ifs" about the future, guide her to notice and then decrease her catastrophizing (fearing the worst).

- Then redirect her to focus on the present moment. Over time, learning to become mindful about the present will naturally make the future seem less important.

- In particular, help your teen challenge the idea that any single situation is absolutely critical for his future. Many teens imagine that success is a linear path from success to success, while for most people the path is often a zigzag, with some failures and regroupings.

Leaving the Nest

Going off to college or living on their own for the first time is a big transition for most teens. Still trying to forge their identity, teens are grappling with who they are and how to move forward with their life, given all the choices they face. In addition, most teens feel unprepared for the increased responsibility and ambivalent about the tremendous changes ahead. Especially before your teen has actually faced these new challenges on her own, she is in something of a "no man's land," having left the past but not yet faced the future, squarely in between dependence and independence.

Ryan was suddenly anxious in the summer before he went to college. He questioned if he had made the right choice for college and began second-guessing his career goals. He worried about what it would be like to have a roommate and whether he would make new friends. It seemed daunting to have to speak with a college professor or take a college exam. He doubted that he was ready for this change.

If your teen, like Ryan, is experiencing anxiety about the transition to adulthood, here are some ways to help:

- Before she leaves home, make sure that your teen practices the skills she will need for managing her day-to-day responsibilities, such as being able to speak to a teacher or doctor, manage money, and organize her day. If your teen is anxious about performing those activities, see Chapter 4 for strategies to create a challenge ladder to practice these goals.

- As your teen begins this transition, encourage him to not judge success by an irrational standard of "all or nothing," but instead notice areas of strength and areas needing improvement.

- The human brain does not fully mature until the mid-twenties, which may cause some bumps along the road toward full independence. Make sure not to expect perfect maturity and success too quickly; instead, express confidence in your teen's resourcefulness to work through challenges, despite some hiccups along the way.

- Encourage your teen to set small goals (for behaviors, not outcomes) and to self-reward when achieving them. This will help your teen to monitor his behavior, make adjustments over time, and focus on areas that he can control.

- Keep the lines of communication open, but gradually decrease parental efforts to step in and solve problems. Be present and ready to help but not over-controlling. Your teen and soon-to-be young adult will experience greater confidence as she gradually learns to handle challenges on her own.

> Deliberately notice and acknowledge positive and healthy ways that your teen solves problems and copes with challenges. This will help reinforce her efforts over time to be a confident problem solver.

Activity: My Teen's Anxiety Flashpoints

What are the anxiety flashpoints in your teen's life? Consider the triggers of stress and upcoming transitions and write them down. Then, using the tips in this chapter as a guideline, begin to think about a few proactive ways to intervene for each flashpoint. Your efforts may reduce unhealthy levels of anxiety or, in the best case, even prevent them altogether.

Maintaining an Anxiety-Busting Lifestyle

Managing anxiety in general through the teen years involves acting like a ship's captain; working hard to guide the boat to calm waters and avoiding the rocky bottom whenever you can. The problem, though, as most parents notice, is that now teens are often the ones steering the ship! Despite their greater independence and desire to make their own choices, teens still need a certain level of structure in order to thrive. Here are some quick tips for promoting an anxiety-busting lifestyle through the teen years:

- Support the value of downtime, recreation, and play. Overstressed and overscheduled teens need time to recharge their batteries.

- Foster socialization and social support. Research confirms the value of social support in reducing anxiety and increasing resilience to stress. Encourage your teen to develop a supportive peer group.

- Anxiety can worsen with fatigue, which tends to make irrational thoughts more noticeable and less easy to challenge. Your teen will do better with a consistent bedtime (ideally eight to nine hours of nightly sleep) and a limit on electronics close to bedtime.

- Limit electronics if they are having a negative impact. Observe the effects that video games, computer games, and apps have on your teen. If you notice an increase in irritability, anxiety, sleep deprivation, or social withdrawal, set up a structure around electronics (when to start and stop and when to take breaks).

- Monitor the impact of social media. Some teens constantly compare their (and their friends') social status on social media. This can worsen worry and social fears. If this is your teen, help her consider the impact of her relationship with social media, and encourage a change.

- Maintain positive, affectionate communication in the family, which will help to reduce overall stress.

When Anxiety Becomes a Significant Concern

So far in this chapter, we've discussed typical times when a teen might experience anxiety. By now you'll know that you should expect the occasional anxious moment as a normal part of adolescence. Usually, such anxiety stays at a mild level or subsides in time. But sometimes anxiety lingers or even gets worse. The next section will tell you how to spot the signs of a developing anxiety problem and, if a disorder has developed, learn how to help.

Spotting the Signs of a Problem

How can you tell when anxiety is out of the range of the normal ups and downs of adolescence and has become a cause for concern? Here are six potential signs:

- Your teen seems significantly distressed (she appears anxious or says she is).

- Your teen's behavior has changed markedly (such as avoidance or modifying usual routines).

- Your teen's everyday school functioning is impaired (there are indicators such as lowered grades, incomplete work, inattention, or a change in classroom behavior).

- Your teen's participation in social situations has decreased (you observe increased social isolation or reduced participation in activities).

- Your teen is having trouble bouncing back from minor setbacks (the fears are out of proportion to the situation).

- Your teen exhibits additional symptoms beyond simple anxiety (such as trouble concentrating, irritability, sleep disturbance, muscle tension, fatigue, stomachache, or dizziness).

The more signs of anxiety your teen is experiencing, the more likely he is experiencing a clinically significant level of anxiety, with symptoms severe enough to cause significant distress and impairment in his life. With transitory anxiety—the kind that comes and goes—fears are reasonable, expected given the situation, and developmentally appropriate, and they decrease in intensity over time. Problematic anxiety is disproportionate to the situation, grows over time, and often has generalized quite a bit beyond the original situation.

Activity: Could Anxiety Have Become a Disorder?

Ask yourself these questions to consider whether your teen might be suffering from an anxiety disorder:

☐   Does my teen appear distressed?

☐   Does my teen report feeling anxious?

☐   Is my teen showing significant avoidance?

☐   Is my teen showing other changes in behavior?

☐   Is there evidence of a change in school performance?

☐   Is there evidence of a change in socialization?

☐   Is my teen struggling to bounce back from an everyday challenge?

☐   Are there signs of a concentration problem?

☐   Are there signs of increased irritability?

☐   Are there signs of worsened sleep?

☐   Are there signs of worsened physical discomfort?

If your teen is demonstrating one or more of these problems, consider seeking professional help to further understand what might be going on and how to address it. Keep in mind, the principles in this book for managing anxiety (such as challenging thoughts and using exposure to overcome avoidance) that you have learned to apply will help your teen, whether he is in treatment or not.

Types of Anxiety Disorders Common in Teens

Anxiety disorders are named for the symptoms that are apparent. *Generalized anxiety disorder* involves persistent worry about a wide variety of things. We can think of this disorder as an example of worry "gone wild"—too much worry about too many things! A number of anxiety disorders are named for the patient's specific worry or problem. *Social anxiety disorder* is manifested by intense fears about being judged negatively in social situations. *Separation anxiety disorder* concerns worry about separation from caregivers. While panic attacks can accompany any anxiety disorder, *panic disorder* is named for persistent worry about having panic attacks. Often accompanying panic symptoms is *agoraphobia*, a fear and avoidance of being in certain places. Lastly, *specific phobias* are about having an intense fear of a specific object or situation.

Two remaining disorders that can trigger anxiety are unique in their development. In *post-traumatic stress disorder*, first the person experiences or witnesses a terrifying traumatic or life-threatening event; then symptoms develop as a result of this trauma. Lastly, in *obsessive-compulsive disorder* there are unwanted and intrusive thoughts (obsessions), which the person responds to with compulsions (urges to do something in response to those thoughts).

Again, in all of these cases, a worry or fear is not enough to diagnose a disorder. The disorder is diagnosed when there are accompanying symptoms as well as significant distress or impairment. Keep in mind also that there are disorders that are not anxiety disorders but can include anxiety as a feature. For example, *adjustment disorder*, brought on by an excessive reaction to a life stressor, can include anxiety as a prominent feature. Certain medical conditions can also lead to an anxiety disorder. Appendix C provides a more detailed description of the anxiety disorders diagnosed in children and adolescents.

Seeking Help

Despite your best efforts, anxiety may be having too great an impact on your teen. If so, it is time to address the problem with an action plan. If you suspect that your teen is suffering from an anxiety disorder that needs treatment, there are a number of helpful options.

First, research shows that cognitive behavioral therapy (CBT), the principles of which serve as a foundation for this book, is highly effective in treating all of the anxiety disorders. You can find good cognitive behavioral therapists that serve teens in your community by asking a pediatrician, guidance counselor, or psychiatrist for a referral. Searching online for "cognitive behavioral therapy," "anxiety," and your local area can also be the start (not the end) of your search.

When you find a few names of therapists with good reputations, be sure to check their experience and credentials in treating anxiety disorders, as well as their experience serving an adolescent population and working with families. Therapists who specialize in child and adolescent psychology often add great value through their specific knowledge and expertise. In addition, if you are aware that your teen is suffering from a particular anxiety disorder, make sure the therapist has sufficient expertise in treating that particular problem and can briefly articulate his or her approach to treating the problem. Lastly, don't forget that seeking therapy for yourself can be very beneficial as an avenue for support, reflection, and advice on how to cope with an anxious teen or cope with your own anxiety.

Questions to Ask a Potential Therapist

- How many years have you been in clinical practice?

- What is your approach or orientation to treatment?

- Do you have specific training in anxiety disorder treatment?

- Do you have experience and training in working with children and teens?

- Do you frequently treat what my teen is experiencing?

- How will you approach treatment with my teen?

- Do you involve parents? If so, how?

When researching the best therapist to help your teen, it can be helpful to keep track of the answers to these questions. A downloadable worksheet is available at http://www.newharbinger.com/34657. (See the back of the book for more information.)

The combination of therapy and medication to treat anxiety disorders often works best to alleviate symptoms. However, many teens can benefit from therapy alone. In fact, as this book discusses, since avoidance strengthens fears, a teen treated solely with psychotropic drugs may need a concurrent CBT treatment plan to reduce any behavioral avoidance. The combination often produces striking improvement. If your teen is working with a therapist, that professional can help determine when a referral to a psychiatrist might be indicated.

> Along with significant distress and significant dysfunction, the inability to bounce back from hardships can be an important sign of problematic anxiety.

Signs That Positive Change Is Happening

Once your teen has begun to practice a positive self-help plan to decrease anxiety (as this book outlines) or has begun treatment, you naturally will want to know whether the critical change you're hoping for is occurring. It's helpful to consider a few key markers of change. First, is your teen gradually experiencing less distress when facing situations that typically provoke anxiety? Second, since anxious teens often have developed a pattern of avoiding challenges, you should see those avoidance behaviors gradually decreasing as well. Third, your teen's response to new anxiety-provoking situations that he has never encountered before can measure the state of his anxiety. Does he display more realistic thinking and better coping with new stressors? Does he move toward positive goals and take new risks? Remember to give your teen's efforts a chance to work before assessing these factors.

Some teens proceed quickly and successfully to demonstrate positive behavior change; others need extra time to absorb and practice new ways of thinking and behaving. If your teen is suffering from more than one psychiatric condition (such as depression as well), then a change in behavior might take longer. Most teens who consistently practice the strategies discussed in this book have the potential to make great strides in alleviating their anxiety. As a bonus, in the process they learn a new way of interacting with their anxiety, which paves the way for greater resiliency and helps to prevent future relapses.

10 A Roadmap for Parents

Coping with an Anxious Teen, Challenging Your Worries, and Leading the Way

Emma's Story: Finding a New Path

At first it was so difficult. I was so worn out, concerned for my daughter, and frankly frustrated. Lindsey leaned on me constantly for all sorts of things, but eventually I held firm and explained that this was making her anxiety worse and that we both needed to change how we were approaching things. I needed to stop being so worried about how anxiety was hurting her, and she needed to stop following her first instinct to rush and escape from it. I gradually saw a difference, but what made me so proud was when she really decided to see me more as a support to help her face her fears than as a crutch to help her avoid them. I know that I had helped her get to this point with the changes that I made, which of course I am still working on. We both went through some challenging times facing up to anxiety, but now I know that she will be okay.

Helping Parents Cope

We know the huge impact that maladaptive anxiety in teens has on them, but what about parents? The journey for parents is in many ways no less difficult and no less important. This chapter focuses on how you, as a parent, can cope with your teen's anxiety, in a way that helps both you and your teen.

As any parent of an anxious teen knows, parenting your teen in the midst of an anxious episode is not for the fainthearted! If you had a thermometer that could measure the impact that your teen's anxiety has on you and your family, how high would the rating go—just a little elevated, moderately high, or maybe, at times, sky high? Here are just a few ways that anxiety in your teen can have an adverse impact on you:

- It can make communicating with your teen a challenge.

- It can cause your teen to be defiant at times, due to her anxiety.

- It can cause disagreements between you and your partner about how to deal with the anxiety.

- It can make it difficult to have quality time for yourself.

- It can make life unpredictable, since anxiety can flare up unexpectedly.

- It can cause you or other family members to be constantly pulled into helping your teen.

- It can cause you to make adjustments in household routines.

- It can cause your teen, you, and your family to miss out on important events.

On top of all the everyday hardships that anxiety causes, teen anxiety can trigger multiple challenging emotions in the parents. For example, parents may worry about how their teen is coping, feel sad at how anxiety is getting in the way of their teen's life, experience guilt for somehow "causing" the anxiety, feel angry for the way their teen is acting up, and feel discouraged when nothing seems to take away the anxiety. Over time, all of these emotional consequences of anxiety can have an impact on you, and that, in turn, also may not be so good for your teen. For example, research shows that when a parent suffers from significant anxiety, children with anxiety disorders tend to do worse.

So when you decrease the impact that your teen's anxiety has on you and focus on your own emotional health, this will help your teen as well. Recent research by Golda Ginsburg and her colleagues at Johns Hopkins also encouragingly suggests that by applying CBT principles to decrease your teen's anxiety and modifying how you respond to your teen, you could even prevent your teen's developing an anxiety disorder. In this study, the onset of anxiety disorders over a twelve-month period was almost seven times lower for children of parents who implemented a cognitive behavioral intervention for anxiety.

In the sections that follow, I'll give you an eight-point plan to make the journey of caring for your anxious teen less stressful and more positive, for both you and your teen. You'll focus on exploring whether your thoughts, beliefs, and expectations about your teen's anxiety are beneficial or detrimental to you and your teen. Then, to manage the stress of caring for an anxious teen, you'll work on maintaining an optimistic outlook, increasing your social support, and reserving time for self-care. Finally, you'll set some limits on the way anxiety has taken over your relationship with your teen and practice modeling a new way forward. Altogether, this plan will keep both you and your teen on a path toward positive change.

> Recent research suggests that by applying CBT principles to decrease your teen's anxiety and modifying how you respond to your teen, you could potentially prevent your teen's developing an anxiety disorder.

1. Tame Your Anxious Thoughts

Most parents worry a great deal about how anxiety is affecting their teen. These worries make it harder to cope with anxious teens and can get in the way of making effective parenting decisions in a difficult moment. As this book emphasizes, the best way to tame worries is to *challenge anxious thoughts*. Just like their anxious teens who have negative and catastrophic thoughts, parents can get similar thoughts when worrying about their teen's anxiety. In fact, since anxiety often runs in families, parents may be suffering from a tendency to be anxious and worry as well. Here are some examples of thoughts parents report having when they observe anxiety in their teen:

- *If she can't cope with challenges now, she will never be able to handle herself in the future.*

- *If he doesn't start losing his shyness, he won't have any friends.*

- *She can't handle another panic attack. She will fall apart.*

Catch yourself the next time your negative thoughts take on a life of their own. Consider whether your thoughts are tending to the extreme and might not be taking in the full facts of the situation. Here are some examples of more realistic thoughts to substitute for the ones just listed:

- *Just because he is struggling a bit now doesn't mean it will last forever. He has gotten through other challenges before.*

- *Although she might have trouble maintaining some of her friendships, she still has people who enjoy her company, and she can get better in time.*

- *He's been coping with uncomfortable feelings and can tolerate them.*

When teens hear their parents expressing negative and catastrophic thoughts, it can sometimes set off a feedback loop, causing the teens' perceptions to worsen as well. Conversely, challenging your own anxious thoughts models for your teen how to do the same.

Activity: Challenging My Worries

Now that you have learned how your teen can challenge his faulty thinking, you can practice working on your own anxious thoughts as well. Ask yourself the following questions to challenge your worries next time your teen is having an anxious moment (try to do it in the moment, when you have direct access to those thoughts, rather than trying to recall them later):

- What is going through my mind right now?

- What specific thoughts am I thinking?

- Am I focusing only on the negative or assuming only the worst that could happen?

- Looking at all of the evidence about how my teen is doing, how realistic are these thoughts?

- What can I think instead that is a more realistic way of viewing the situation?

For example, you might think, *It is useless. She is not getting better at all. Nothing is working.* Then look at the evidence: she used successful strategies yesterday and has been improving gradually over time, despite setbacks. New thought: *She is having a setback right now, but judging by her positive change in behavior over time, some of the strategies have worked.*

---

2. Change Beliefs About Parenting and Anxiety

An insightful parent recently said to me, "I spend all of my time making sure everyone else is happy. And unless my children are happy, I can't be happy. I know this is not healthy, but I can't seem to stop." As this parent fully realized, this is a no-win situation, since we can't keep our kids happy all the time! Even more so when it comes to facing anxiety: for teens to get better, parents must learn to tolerate their teens' sometimes being unhappy, anxious, and uncomfortable.

Our beliefs about parenting hold the key to how we perceive many interactions with our children; unfortunately, sometimes these beliefs are too rigid. One indicator that you might be holding rigid beliefs is if you think in terms of absolutes, such as "never" or "always." You might also be applying strict rules to your behavior, evidenced simply by what you believe you "must" do or "should" do. Parents have acknowledged holding overly rigid beliefs about their role as a parent in helping their anxious teen, such as the following:

- "I always should do everything to reduce my teen's distress."

- "I should be able to fix my teen's anxiety problem."

- "I should prevent my teen from experiencing any risk of harm or failure."

When you recognize faulty beliefs like these, you should question them. Of course parents can guide their teens in overcoming anxiety, but they can't fix their teen's anxiety problem for them, nor can they (nor should they attempt to) prevent their teen's distress. To overcome anxiety, teens also have to face up to the possibility of things not working out, and they shouldn't be protected from risks or failure—situations that can offer important learning experiences.

On top of having those parenting beliefs, many parents seem to hold their own problematic beliefs about the nature of anxiety. Remember the discussion in Chapter 4 about the anxiety misconceptions held by many teens? Parents also often have their own such misconceptions; for example:

- "Anxiety is harmful to my teen."

- "My teen should be completely free of anxiety."

Holding on to misconceptions like these actually makes it more difficult for parents to help their teen confront their fears and tolerate their teen's being anxious. Anxiety can serve many useful functions. It can increase motivation (such as during an important test) or can signal a challenge or risk ahead that we need to prepare for. Just as teens need to realize that anxiety is not harmful and that it can even be adaptive in the right amounts, parents need to accept this new way of looking at anxiety as well.

It takes time and effort to identify your beliefs about anxiety and your role as a parent in addressing it. However, identifying such beliefs is an important first step to making sure that your beliefs don't get in the way of your supporting your teen to manage her anxiety. The next time your teen has a day punctuated by high anxiety, explore the meaning of this by asking yourself *And that means?* or *What does this mean about me as a parent?* This will help you to uncover any hidden and unnecessary assumptions that you might have about your role or about anxiety itself. You might root out unhealthy and unproductive beliefs, such as *This means my teen's anxiety is my fault* or *This means my teen is not trying hard to change, otherwise the anxiety would be gone.* If you discover any beliefs that don't view anxiety or your role as a parent realistically, make a point of challenging them. Healthy beliefs sustain your well-being and coping efforts and make it easier for you and your teen to work together to challenge fears.

It is important to expect and be accepting of the occasional relapse. Rather than seeing relapses as an all-or-nothing failure to cope, see them as a sign that your teen needs to pause and reevaluate, learn more skills, or practice skills already learned.

3. Set Realistic Expectations for Change

Much of the frustration of dealing with anxious teens arises when you set expectations for change too high, for both yourself and your teen. Regarding expectations for yourself, many parents feel guilty that they somehow caused their teen to be anxious, or feel that they should be able to quickly assuage their teen's anxiety. Or they may choose to believe that persistent anxiety can be eliminated quickly. Of course, none of these expectations are realistic, but by having those expectations, parents increase their own distress. Many parents then push their teen to stop feeling anxious as quickly as possible, and they become disappointed, worried, and angry when this doesn't occur. This sets up a negative communication pattern between parent and teen, with teens feeling that parents are demanding a change. In response to this pressure, some teens resist, and others become even more anxious.

Maladaptive anxiety can take time to develop, so it can also take time to dissipate. Teens need time to learn the skills necessary to combat anxiety. Therefore, it is important to reduce your perfectionism when setting goals for reducing anxiety and to see the effort more as a trek up a steep mountain. Every step gets you closer to the top, but sometimes the road is longer than you would wish! It is important to also expect and be accepting of the occasional relapse. Again, rather than seeing relapses as an all-or-nothing failure to cope, see them as a sign that your teen needs to pause and reevaluate their situation. Perhaps your teen needs to learn more skills or just get back to practicing the skills already learned.

Activity: My Expectations

Ask yourself: what are your expectations about your teen's anxiety? For example, do you expect the anxiety to go away quickly? Do you expect your teen to never again become very anxious? Then ask yourself if these expectations are realistic, given what you know or have learned about anxiety through reading this book.

---

4. Notice the Positives

Chapter 2 discussed the advantages of attending to non-anxious behavior as a simple but powerful strategy to decrease anxious behavior. This strategy is important not just for your teen but also for yourself. By noticing the positives and small triumphs along the way, in terms of both what your teen does to change behavior and what you do as well, you will help decrease those catastrophic thoughts that *nothing is working*. Every day, make a point of paying attention to what is working, no matter how small the change in your teen's behavior. Notice instances when:

- Your teen displayed calm behavior in the face of a fear.

- Your teen displayed brave behavior in facing a fear.

- Your teen employed a successful strategy to defeat fears.

- Something you did helped your teen get through an anxious moment.

Activity: Noticing the Positives

It can help to keep a running list of positive moments in a journal that you and your teen experienced on the journey toward a less anxious life. When you are having a rough day, look back at the journal. This will work to keep your spirits up when things look bleak. If your teen experiences a setback, you can also use the list to remind your teen of her own accomplishments in facing her fears.

> Every day, make a point of paying attention to what is working, no matter how small the change in your teen's behavior.

5. Seek Social Support

Research suggests that social support is good medicine for both body and mind. Parents of anxious teens without social support are less able to accurately judge how they and their teen are doing. Instead, they are left wondering, *Is it just the way I am parenting? Is it just my teen?* Yet anxiety and anxiety disorders are common enough in teens that millions of parents share your worries and concerns. Parents can also benefit from the support, empathy, and help with coping that communication with other parents provides.

To get through the day-to-day challenges of dealing with an anxious teen, seek support from a trusted friend, a local support group, parenting groups, or an online forum. It is especially useful to gain perspective from others who have been in your shoes. In addition, it always helps to get away from a stressful environment for a while, so consider participating in book clubs, yoga classes, or other avenues for meeting people and relaxing at the same time. Parents who feel isolated (perhaps even from a coparent who may be unavailable or disagree with your parenting approach) may be more likely to lose their cool with their teen in a stressful moment. Appendix D lists organizations that can also provide education and support to families.

6. *Create Physical and Mental Space for Yourself*

The teen years are usually a time of gradual separation and independence from parents, yet anxiety can play havoc with the normal course of development. Just when most parents expect their teens to be increasingly ready to handle things on their own, anxious teens remain dependent on their parents in numerous ways. Anxious teens rely heavily on their parents by:

- Seeking excess reassurance or advice

- Requesting help with doing things that they wish to avoid doing (such as speaking on the teen's behalf, opening doors, or picking up objects)

- Requesting the time and physical presence of their parents to cope with difficult situations (such as staying physically close or attending outside events)

- Requiring a parent to change household routines (such as checking locks, washing laundry in a certain way, or participating in a lengthy bedtime ritual)

Altogether, these are significant and persistent demands on parents' time, energies, and emotions. Even worse, by parents providing all of this support, there is a gradual loss of personal boundary between parent and child, which can make a parent feel frustrated and trapped. If your answer to the question, *When have I focused on me lately?* is *Me? Oh, I'd forgotten about myself,* then there is a problem!

Amid the exhausting blur of helping your anxious teen, it is especially important to not neglect your own needs and personal identity. Parents of anxious teens are used to being interrupted and setting aside their own needs to attend to their teen. If this sounds familiar, begin to carve out some space and time in which your teen is not the central focus of your life. Next, identify something that you particularly enjoy and schedule time to focus on it. Discovering a new passion or rediscovering a long-lost passion can be both fulfilling and stress-relieving.

Parents who do this have to get past feelings of guilt that they are somehow being "selfish" for focusing on themselves. However, once they start, it becomes a refreshing and energizing experience that helps them to better function as parents. Perhaps as your child or preteen got older you had begun to have some time for yourself, but as anxiety hit during the teen years, you had to backtrack and become more vigilant again. Or, if your teen developed anxiety when she was quite young, she may have always relied on you excessively to help her cope. Now, with this book's message about what works, you can regroup and reevaluate the role you play in helping your teen.

A growing body of research shows that certain parenting practices—such as parental overprotection, over-control, and reinforcement of avoidance behavior—are associated with (although do not necessarily cause) increased anxiety in children, so reducing how much you step in may pay off for both you and your teen. Gradually, over time, begin to set limits with your teen about when and how he can come to you for support. As discussed, we want to move teens toward reducing avoidance and excessive reassurance-seeking so that they become more independent and capable in dealing with their anxiety, which will help both of you.

Convey this message to your teen by encouraging her to see that anxiety shouldn't rule her life, your life, or the functioning of the entire household. Then tell her what you will no longer be doing, and don't forget to explain what she should be doing instead. For example, a mom encouraged her teen to come up with some good ways to talk back to her anxiety on her own, which helped her teen stop waking her mom up in the middle of the night to seek reassurance and a sense of safety. This allowed both of them to finally get a good night's sleep! Another mom, whose teen had a fear of germs, told her son that she would stop opening doors for him. This allowed him to begin to conquer his fears and his mother to not be constantly interrupted to perform this service for him. Again, to do this successfully you have to be willing to tolerate your teen's initially being quite upset and afraid, as well as upset with you! Over time, though, you will restore things to the way they are supposed to be between a parent and teen child—with some support, but a gradually increasing independence.

> If your teen developed anxiety when she was quite young, she may have always relied on you excessively to help her cope. With this book's message about what works, you can regroup and reevaluate your role in helping your teen.

Activity: Time for Myself

Check in with yourself about how often you are stepping in to help your teen in areas where (1) your teen already has the ability to cope with a challenging situation or (2) in order to become less anxious, your teen needs to practice coping with a challenge on her own. Then gradually step in less often. Once that plan is in motion, begin asking yourself questions such as, *What would I like to get back to, or try, now that I am stepping in less to help my teen?* Ideally, find a passion or absorbing pursuit that you can develop and turn to in times of stress.

7. Find Ways to Quiet Your Mind and Body

Even if you don't tend to experience anxiety in general, having your child's anxiety act up severely, frequently, or at the drop of a hat can frazzle anyone's nerves. It's not just teens who are vulnerable—we *all* have an internal alarm system that can go off when we feel under threat. To reduce anxiety's impact, we have to pay attention to our own nervous system as well.

Ask yourself: *When was the last time I felt really calm?* Again, if it has not been for a while, this is a cause for concern! During times of stress, it may be that our typical coping mechanisms just aren't up to the task of soothing us. Normally resilient and strong parents have reported gradual loss of sleep, increased irritability, increased muscle tension, and even panic symptoms, as the stress of dealing with an anxious teen wears them down. And if you are predisposed to anxiety, the stress of seeing your own teen become anxious might have triggered your anxiety to reappear or worsen.

Chapter 8 discusses some ways to calm the body and mind down, such as with belly breathing, meditation, and general mindfulness strategies (see also Appendix E for apps that might help with this). In addition to those strategies, focus on ways to reduce your overall stress level. This means taking steps to mitigate unnecessary stress whenever possible.

At the height of your teen's anxiety, you might need to give up some things you are doing for others that are unnecessary or add to the time pressure you feel. Ask yourself whether you need to modify some of your methods for coping with stress. Don't forget about your own "perpetual anxiety cycle." How you think about and respond to your own anxiety will determine whether it calms down quickly or even goes away. When you are feeling a sense of inner calm, you will be better able to demonstrate outward calm and supportive behavior the next time your teen's anxiety flares up. The alternative is risking an escalation in both your teen's anxiety and your own stress and anxiety, as they interact and worsen.

Activity: A Parent's Stress Check

Ask yourself the following questions to determine if you need to change your coping strategies for dealing with stress:

- How often do I feel very stressed out? One day a week, a few days, or every day?

- What is my baseline level of stress (my average daily level of stress from 1 to 10), and what would I like it to be?

- Do the coping strategies that I use help to decrease my stress most of the time, some of the time, or only rarely?

- Do I need to use these coping strategies more often?

- Do I need to change my coping strategies?

- If you answered yes to the last question, think of one new coping strategy that you could use.

We rarely stop and think about whether the plan we have for coping is working, so doing a stress check will help you to make any necessary changes. A downloadable worksheet is available at http://www.newharbinger.com/34657. (See the back of the book for more information.)

---

8. Take the Long View About Your Role

When you are right in the middle of a challenging time, it may seem impossible to stop and consider the journey you and your teen are on. But stepping back to do so will help you gain a better perspective on your role as a parent of an anxious teen. So often, parents feel helpless and self-critical when anxiety arises in their teen and their efforts to help just don't seem to work.

When it seems like you're just putting out one fire after another, it is time to take the long view in judging your job as the parent of an anxious teen. That means to consider what long-term factors are important and what you can do *over time* to help your teen get better. To begin with, when you continue to practice empathizing with your teen's struggles, you become a more effective communicator with your teen over time and strengthen your relationship with him. Now that you know the power of modifying anxious thinking, rather than giving advice, you fundamentally change the way you and your teen relate to each other when anxiety hits. You can also make it a long-term goal to eliminate anxious avoidance and to make sure you don't inadvertently reward that behavior. In the long run, this guidance will teach your teen a model for challenging and facing fears that will reap large rewards.

Most importantly, never forget the critical job you perform as a role model for putting anxiety in its place. When you model how a person can manage anxiety, by showing rather than telling, you convey gradually over time a *blueprint* for how problematic anxiety can be managed and defeated. We have discussed modeling all along as a way of improving different facets of anxiety. Putting it all together, here are eight wonderful ways to model a new way of dealing with anxiety:

- Show how to analyze your thinking and challenge faulty thoughts when needed.

- Show how you don't take repetitive or unproductive worries seriously.

- Show how you move to focusing on your goals rather than your worries.

- Show a healthy sense of approaching challenges rather than avoiding them.

- Show tolerance for uncertainty and taking reasonable risks.

- Demonstrate step-by-step problem solving for managing realistic problems.

- Show how you behave as a positive striver and tolerate imperfection.

- Show how you practice self-care and take time to relax your body and mind.

Even when you don't meet the ideals embodied in being the "perfect" role model (which of course no one is), practice self-compassion. Just like your teen, you may have moments where you are at less than your best. As one teen recently expressed, "My mom got really stressed out with some of the stuff I was doing and went over to the dark side!" When these times inevitably occur, you can even use it as a lighthearted teaching moment for your teen. For example, you can say, "Well, I guess my worries got the best of me today. Time to hit the reset button." Taking the long view will help convey to your teen that we judge success or failure not by what happens in any given moment, but by whether we are moving in the right direction.

Changing the Mind Changes the Brain

In the past twenty-five years, a developing body of research has suggested something amazing: changing how your mind works actually changes the brain! These studies demonstrate that CBT alters brain function in those with many types of anxiety disorders (and some other disorders, such as depression, as well), and these changes are similar to the effects of psychotropic drugs. Imagine that! Just learning to think and behave differently changes the way that our brains work. Now research is proving that there is no such thing as a separation between body and mind.

Getting back to the adolescent brain, remember that your teen is still undergoing brain change, which won't be complete until she is about twenty-five. So you have a window of opportunity to affect this process. When parents help anxious teens learn to change a thought and practice a new behavior, they are essentially fostering the same change that occurs during psychotherapy—and doing it when it is really needed, in the moment, when a problem is actually occurring. These changes might even affect the teen brain itself in positive and long-lasting ways. That means you have a privileged and uncommon opportunity to help set your teen on a positive and healthy path. With the new knowledge you have gained about what really works to overcome anxiety, and with your teen's determination and commitment to try something new, there can be great changes ahead.

Acknowledgments

Thank you to my many mentors who trained me in the amazing art and science of psychology as well as specifically in CBT. I have been privileged to learn from national experts in the field of anxiety disorder treatment; I thank you all immensely for your wisdom and guidance. Thanks especially to Dr. Aureen Pinto Wagner, Dr. Martin Franklin, Dr. Eric Storch, and Dr. Alec Pollard. Your training increased my understanding of anxiety treatment by leaps and bounds.

I thank the team at New Harbinger for helping me develop this project from start to finish. First, thank you to Wendy Millstine, acquisitions editor, for enthusiastically believing in the idea for this book. To Vicraj Gill, associate editor, it was a privilege to gain your wonderful insights into how to make the book better, and it brought the book to a whole new level of clarity and meaning. To Melissa Valentine, acquisitions editor, your editorial advice always steered me in the right direction. Thank you, Kristi Hein, for your graceful and artistic editorial efforts. Thank you to Clancy Drake, editorial manager, who guided the book toward excellence.

I am grateful to my friends and family who supported me through this effort. Thank you, Eileen Kennedy-Moore, for providing the spark to help me truly get this project going and being generous with your guidance and wisdom. I was privileged to have my friend and mentor, renowned child psychologist, and the most selfless person I know, Dr. Tamerra Moeller, edit the manuscript word by word and impart her amazing clinical wisdom along the way. I am forever indebted to you for your support. Thank you to my sister, Rajani Wilson, for helping me every step of the way with your advice, editing, and encouragement. To my colleagues Karen Cohen, Carol Blum, Wendy Matthews, and Laura Berness—I appreciate your helpful advice.

One message of this book is that powerful change can happen when we are brave and step into the unknown. I learned this message early on from my father, Dr. B. R. Achar, who left his homeland and traveled to Canada on a dream. He showed me how success comes from dedication, perseverance, and being willing to push yourself to try new challenges. I doubt I would have become an author or a psychologist without his amazing example. My mother, Malathi Achar, showed me the power of being selfless, loving, calm, and practical. She has always been there for me during the most challenging times, which led me to where I am today. Thank you both for your love and support. Thank you to my husband, Jon, for your encouragement and belief in me. To Naveen, my brother, I appreciate your always encouraging me to write a book. To my teen son—your greatest strength is your love of learning, which will take you far through everything that you do. And seeing you move through challenges with great perseverance, bravery, and determination makes me so proud of who you are in this moment and excited for who you will become.

Lastly, thanks to the teens and their parents who put their trust in me to be part of their team in defeating anxiety. It has been a great joy to see your efforts pay off in powerful ways.

APPENDIX A

Socratic Questions

Parents' Easy Guide to Questioning Anxious Thoughts

The following are sample questions to identify worries and gently redirect your teen's anxious thoughts to more realistic and adaptive thoughts. Each goal is followed by a question parents can ask their teens. Remember, easy does it! Wait for a time when your teen's anxiety is not at its peak, and don't overwhelm your teen with too many questions.

Goal: Identify anxious thoughts

- What are your fears or worries saying?

- What is going through your mind right now?

Goal: Encourage testing out worries

- Are there facts that suggest your worries may not be true?

- What is the evidence for and against your worry?

Goal: Identify catastrophizing

- Could you be fearing the worst possible result or outcome?

Goal: Decrease catastrophizing

- Do you have evidence that it will happen, or is this a fear?

- How likely is it to really happen, and what could happen instead?

- Are there ways that the situation is less risky or bad than it seems?

- Could the situation feel less important over time?

Goal: Reduce a one-sided focus on the negative

- Are there any positives to the situation that counteract the negatives?

- What is another way to look at it?

Goal: Decreasing black-and-white thinking

- What is a way of seeing the situation as not all good or all bad but in between?

Goal: Decreasing the mind-reading assumption that people are thinking of you negatively

- What evidence do you have that they are really thinking this about you?

- What could they be thinking of you that might not be so bad?

Goal: Decrease overgeneralizing one negative event to the future

- Could other things happen to make this event less important?

- What might happen instead?

Goal: Foster healthy perspective, positive coping, and problem-solving

- If what you fear really happens, could it be less bad than you think?

- If what you fear really happens, could you be able to handle it?

- Are there some ways to manage or cope with the problem so that it is not so bad?

APPENDIX B
Cognitive Errors

Common Errors in Thinking*

- *All-or-nothing thinking:* Viewing situations in black-and-white extremes, as either good or bad, perfect or a failure.

- *Mental filtering:* Noticing only the negatives.

- *Disqualifying the positive:* Completely discounting positive events when they occur.

- *Mind reading:* Jumping to the conclusion that someone perceives you negatively.

- *Catastrophizing:* Fearing the worst.

- *Overgeneralization:* Drawing a broad conclusion based on a single event or single piece of evidence. In particular, viewing a single event as a sign of a continuing pattern of defeat.

---

* Based on Aaron T. Beck's development of the concept of thinking errors and on David D. Burns's description of the concept in his book *Feeling Good: The New Mood Therapy.*

APPENDIX C
Anxiety Disorders Diagnosed in Children and Adolescents

These are the clinical disorders common to children and adolescents that are associated with anxiety.* As discussed in Chapter 9, anxiety alone is not sufficient to diagnose the disorder; this requires both significant distress and impairment in functioning. The disorders are listed in order from the most common to the least common in adolescents.

Specific Phobia

This disorder involves a strong fear of a specific object or situation, such as flying, animals, vomiting, injections, or seeing blood. Adolescents will avoid the object or situation or endure it with distress, even though the fear is out of proportion to the actual danger involved. About 16 percent of adolescents experience this disorder.

Social Anxiety Disorder

Adolescents with this disorder fear acting in embarrassing ways that they think will result in social disapproval. They will avoid social

---

* Adapted from the *Diagnostic and Statistical Manual of Mental Disorders*, fifth edition, American Psychiatric Association, 2013. Prevalence data also based on National Institute of Mental Health data.

situations in which there is a possibility of disapproval or endure them with distress. There is also anticipatory anxiety about future disapproval. It is commonly diagnosed for the first time in mid- to late adolescence. About 7 percent of adolescents suffer from social anxiety disorder, and the median age of onset is at the start of adolescence (thirteen years).

Post-Traumatic Stress Disorder

Adolescents with PTSD have experienced or witnessed a traumatic event that involved actual or threatened death or injury. In response to this trauma, there can be intense fear, physiological distress, recurrent distressing memories or dreams of the event, and avoidance of anything that reminds one of the trauma. There are also mood changes, cognitive changes, and other symptoms. Due to the trauma, teens may fear being different and not fitting in. Symptoms usually begin within the first three months of the trauma but can have a delayed onset. About 4 percent of teens suffer from this disorder.

Panic Disorder

Adolescents with this disorder experience recurrent unexpected panic attacks that involve a sudden rush of uncomfortable physical sensations. They then worry about having more attacks, think that they are under terrible threat during an attack, and may significantly modify their behavior to avoid more attacks. Panic disorder is very rare in childhood, but the rate of panic disorder gradually increases during adolescence to about 3 percent.

Obsessive-Compulsive Disorder

Adolescents with OCD experience recurrent thoughts, urges, or images that cause anxiety. In response to these obsessions, the adolescent tries to ignore or suppress the thoughts or engages in compulsions, which are repetitive behaviors or mental acts aimed at preventing or reducing anxiety or preventing a feared event from occurring. Common obsessions include fear of contamination, needing to do things exactly a certain way, or thoughts of harm to self. Common compulsions include hand-washing, putting items in order, checking, counting, and repeating words. About 2 to 3 percent of teens suffer from this disorder. One quarter of cases start by age fourteen, and onset in adolescence can lead to a chronic lifetime course, unless treated.

Separation Anxiety Disorder

Adolescents with this disorder experience excessive and developmentally inappropriate anxiety when anticipating or experiencing separation from home or caregivers (usually a parent). Adolescents worry about loss of a loved one or harm coming to them. The worry may also be about something bad happening (such as being kidnapped or lost) to cause separation. As a result of the worry, symptoms may include refusal to go to school to prevent separation, difficulty being alone, difficulty sleeping away from home or loved ones, nightmares of separation, and physical symptoms arising from fears of separation. This disorder is more common in children, but it can occur in a small subset (1.6 percent) of adolescents. It can be triggered by life stress, including, among other things, loss of a loved one, change of school, or divorce.

Generalized Anxiety Disorder

Adolescents with this disorder experience excessive and uncontrollable worry about a variety of things. Along with the worry there are symptoms that impede everyday functioning, such as restlessness, fatigue, poor concentration, irritability, muscle tension, and poor sleep. Adolescents with this disorder tend to worry about the quality of their school and sports performance and can be perfectionistic and reassurance seeking. Around 1 percent of teens suffer from this disorder, but countless others demonstrate milder worry and associated symptoms that cause significant distress.

APPENDIX D
Professional Associations

These organizations all offer information and education to families.

American Academy of Child and Adolescent Psychiatry
http://www.aacap.org

American Psychiatric Association
http://www.psych.org

American Psychological Association
http://www.apa.org, http://www.apahelpcenter.org

Anxiety and Depression Association of America
http://www.adaa.org

Association for Behavioral and Cognitive Therapies
http://www.abct.org

Children with Attention Deficit Disorder (CHADD)
http://www.chadd.org

International OCD Foundation
http://www.ocfoundation.org

National Alliance on Mental Illness
http://www.nami.org

National Institute of Mental Health
http://www.nimh.nih.gov

APPENDIX E
Useful Apps

These are a few popular apps that teens have reported finding useful for relaxation, mindfulness, and meditation. This is not an endorsement of a particular product; rather, if your teen gravitates toward apps rather than reading a book about it (as most teens these days do), let him try a few of these out and see what works for him. What is most important is that your teen feels that the activity is very simple to do, soothing, and enjoyable enough to repeat frequently.

Breathe2Relax

Buddha's Brain

Calm

Insight Timer

Mindfulness

Pacifica—Anxiety, Stress, and Depression Relief

Stop, Breathe & Think

Zen Friend

Selected References and Recommended Readings

Albano, A. M., and M. F. Detweiler. 2001. "The Developmental and Clinical Impact of Social Anxiety and Social Phobia in Children and Adolescents." In *From Social Anxiety to Social Phobia: Multiple Perspectives*, edited by S. G. Hofmann and P. M. DiBartolo. Boston: Allyn & Bacon.

American Psychiatric Association. 2013. *The Diagnostic and Statistical Manual of Mental Disorders* (5th ed.). Washington, D.C.: American Psychiatric Association.

Amir, N., J. Elias, H. Klumpp, and A. Przeworski. 2003. "Attentional Bias to Threat in Social Phobia: Facilitated Processing of Threat or Difficulty Disengaging Attention from Threat?" *Behaviour Research and Therapy* 41:1325–1335.

Antony, M. M., C. L. Purdon, V. Huta, and R. P. Swinson. 1998. "Dimensions of Perfectionism Across the Anxiety Disorders." *Behaviour Research and Therapy* 36:1143–1154.

A-Tjak, J. G., M. L. Davis, N. Morina, M. B. Powers, J. A. Smits, and P. M. Emmelkamp. 2015. "A Meta-Analysis of the Efficacy of Acceptance and Commitment Therapy for Clinically Relevant Mental and Physical Health Problems." *Psychotherapy and Psychosomatics* 84:30–36.

Beck, A. T., G. Emery, and R. L. Greenberg. 2005. *Anxiety Disorders and Phobias: A Cognitive Perspective*. New York: Basic Books.

Beidel, D. C., C. M. Fink, and S. M. Turner. 1996. "Stability of Anxious Symptomatology in Children." *Journal of Abnormal Child Psychology* 24:257–269.

Blakemore, S., and S. Choudhury. 2006. "Development of the Adolescent Brain: Implications for Executive Function and Social Cognition." *Journal of Child Psychology and Psychiatry* 47:296–312.

Borkovec, T. D., and S. Hu. 1990. "The Effect of Worry on Cardiovascular Response to Phobic Imagery." *Behaviour Research and Therapy* 28:69–73.

Borkovec, T. D., J. D. Lyonfields, S. L. Wiser, and L. Diehl. 1993. "The Role of Worrisome Thinking in the Suppression of Cardiovascular Response to Phobic Imagery." *Behaviour Research and Therapy* 31:321–324.

Borkovec, T. D., W. J. Rayand, and J. Stober. 1998. "Worry: A Cognitive Phenomenon Intimately Linked to Affective, Physiological, and Interpersonal Behavioral Processes." *Cognitive Therapy and Research* 22:561–576.

Borkovec, T. D., and Roemer, L. 1995. "Perceived Functions of Worry Among Generalized Anxiety Disorder Subjects: Distraction from More Emotional Topics?" *Journal of Behavior Therapy and Experimental Psychiatry* 26:25–30.

Burns, D. 2008. *Feeling Good: The New Mood Therapy*. New York: Avon.

Burstein, M., and G. S. Ginsburg. 2010. "The Effect of Parental Modeling of Anxious Behaviors and Cognitions in School-Aged Children: An Experimental Pilot Study." *Behaviour Research and Therapy* 48:506–515.

Casey, B. J., J. N. Gïedd, and K. M. Thomas. 2000. "Structural and Functional Brain Development and Its Relation to Cognitive Development." *Biological Psychiatry* 54:241–257.

Clark, D. A., and A. T. Beck. 2010. *Cognitive Therapy of Anxiety Disorders: Science and Practice*. New York: Guilford Press.

Connolly, S. D., G. A. Bernstein, and the Work Group on Quality Issues. 2007. "Practice Parameters for the Assessment and Treatment of Children and Adolescents with Anxiety Disorders." *Journal of the American Academy of Child and Adolescent Psychiatry* 2:267–283.

Costello, E. J., H. L. Egger, and A. Angold. 2005. "The Developmental Epidemiology of Anxiety Disorders: Phenomenology, Prevalence and Comorbidity." *Child and Adolescent Psychiatric Clinics of North America* 14:631–648.

Craske, M. G., M. Treanor, C. C. Conway, T. Zbozinek, and B. Vervliet. 2014. "Maximizing Exposure Therapy: An Inhibitory Learning Approach." *Behaviour Research and Therapy* 58:10–23.

Curry, J. F., J. S. March, and A. S. Hervey. 2004. "Comorbidity of Childhood and Adolescent Anxiety Disorders: Prevalence and Implications." In *Phobic and Anxiety Disorders in Children and Adolescents: A Clinician's Guide to Effective Psychosocial and Pharmacological Interventions*, edited by T. H. Ollendick and J. S. March. New York: Oxford University Press.

Deardorff, J., C. Hayward, K. A. Wilson, S. Bryson, L. Hammer, and S. Agras. 2007. "Puberty and Gender Interact to Predict Social Anxiety Symptoms in Early Adolescence." *Journal of Adolescent Health* 41:102–104.

Dugas, M. J., N. Laugesen, and W. M. Bukowski. 2012. "Intolerance of Uncertainty, Fear of Anxiety, and Adolescent Worry." *Journal of Abnormal Child Psychology* 40:863–870.

Eley, T. C., T. A. McAdams, F. V. Rijsdijk, P. Lichtenstein, J. Narusyte, D. Reiss, E. L. Spotts, J. M. Ganiban, and J. M. Neiderhiser. 2015. "The Intergenerational Transmission of Anxiety: A Children-of-Twins Study." *American Journal of Psychiatry* 172:630–637.

Frewen, P. A., D. J. Dozois, and R.A. Lanius. 2008. "Neuroimaging Studies of Psychological Interventions for Mood and Anxiety Disorders: Empirical and Methodological Review." *Clinical Psychology Review* 28:228–246.

Garcia, A., J. Sapyta, P. Moore, J. Freeman, M. Franklin, J. March, and E. B. Foa. 2010. "Predictors and Moderators of Treatment Outcome in the Pediatric Obsessive Compulsive Treatment Study (POTS1)." *Journal of the American Academy of Child & Adolescent Psychiatry* 10:1024–1033.

Ginsburg, G. S., K. L. Drake, J. Tein, R. Teetsel, and M. A. Riddle. 2015. "Preventing Onset of Anxiety Disorders in Offspring of Anxious Parents: A Randomized Controlled Trial of a Family-Based Intervention." *American Journal of Psychiatry* 172: 1207–1214.

Ginsburg, G. S., and M. C. Schlossberg. 2002. "Family-Based Treatment of Childhood Anxiety Disorders." *International Review of Psychiatry* 14:143–154.

Greene, R. W. 1998. *The Explosive Child.* New York: HarperCollins.

Hayward, C., J. D. Killen, L. D. Hammer, I. F. Litt, D. M. Wilson, B. Simmonds, and C. B. Taylor. 1992. "Pubertal Stage and Panic Attack History in Sixth- and Seventh-Grade Girls." *American Journal of Psychiatry* 149:1239–1243.

Hayward, C., J. D. Killen, and H. C. Kraemer. 2000. "Predictors of Panic Attacks in Adolescents." *Journal of the American Academy of Child and Adolescent Psychiatry* 39:207–214.

Hirsch, C. R., and D. M. Clark. 2004. "Information Processing Bias in Social Phobia." *Clinical Psychology Review* 24:799–825.

Hoffman, S. G., A. T. Sawyer, A. A. Witt, and D. Oh. 2010. "The Effect of Mindfulness-Based Therapy on Anxiety and Depression: A Meta-Analytic Review." *Journal of Consulting and Clinical Psychology* 78:169–183.

Hudson, J. L., C. Newall, R. M. Rapee, H. J. Lyneham, C. C. Schniering, V. M. Wuthrich, S. Schneider, E. Seely-Wait, S. Edwards, and N. S. Gar. 2014. "The Impact of Brief Parental Anxiety Management on Child Anxiety Treatment Outcomes: A Controlled Trial." *Journal of Clinical Child & Adolescent Psychology* 43:370–380.

Hudson, J. L., and R. M. Rapee. 2001. "Parent-Child Interactions and Anxiety Disorders: An Observational Study." *Behaviour Research and Therapy* 39:1411–1427.

Janeck, A. S., and J. E. Calamari. 1999. "Thought Suppression in Obsessive-Compulsive Disorder." *Cognitive Therapy and Research* 23:497–509.

Kendler, K. S., A. C. Heath, N. G. Martin, and L. J. Eaves. 1987. "Symptoms of Anxiety and Symptoms of Depression: Same Genes, Different Environments?" *Archives of General Psychiatry* 44:451–457.

LaGrega, A. M., and N. Shiloff. 1998. "Understanding and Assessing Social Anxiety in Adolescents." *Journal of Abnormal Child Psychology* 26:83–94.

Lebowitz, E. R., K. E. Panza, J. Su, and M. H. Bloch. 2012. "Family Accommodation in Obsessive-Compulsive Disorder." *Expert Review of Neurotherapeutics* 12:229–238.

Lira Yoon, K., and R. E. Zinbarg. 2007. "Threat Is in the Eye of the Beholder: Social Anxiety and the Interpretation of Ambiguous Facial Expressions." *Behaviour Research and Therapy* 45:839–847.

March, J., and H. L. Leonard. 1998. "Obsessive-Compulsive Disorder in Children and Adolescents." In *Obsessive-Compulsive Disorder: Theory, Research, and Treatment,* edited by R. P. Swinson, M. M. Antony, S. Rachman, and M. A. Richter. New York: Guilford Press.

March, J. S., and K. Mulle. 1998. *OCD in Children and Adolescents: A Cognitive-Behavioral Treatment Manual.* New York: Guilford Press.

Mathews, A. 1990. "Why Worry? The Cognitive Function of Anxiety." *Behaviour Research and Therapy* 28:455–468.

McLeod, B. D., J. J. Wood, and S. B. Avny. 2011. "Parenting and Child Anxiety Disorders." In *Handbook of Child and Adolescent Anxiety Disorders,* edited by D. McLay and E. A. Storch. New York: Springer.

Merikangas, K. R., J. P. He, M. Burstein, S. A. Swanson, S. Avenevoli, L. Cui, C. Benjet, K. Georgiases, and J. Swendsen. 2010. "Lifetime Prevalence of Mental Disorders in U.S. Adolescents: Results from the National Cormorbidity Survey Replication—Adolescent Supplement (NCS-A)." *Journal of American Academy of Child & Adolescent Psychiatry* 49:980–989.

Moulding, R., and M. Kyrios. 2006. "Anxiety Disorders and Control Related Beliefs: The Exemplar of Obsessive-Compulsive Disorder (OCD)." *Clinical Psychology Review* 26:573–583.

Ollendick, T. H., and J. S. March. 2004. *Phobic and Anxiety Disorders in Children and Adolescents: A Clinician's Guide to Effective Psychosocial and Pharmacological Interventions.* New York: Oxford University Press.

Piacentini, J., R. L. Bergman, S. Chang, A. Langley, T. Peris, J. Wood., and J. McCracken. 2011. "Controlled Comparison of Family Cognitive Behavioral Therapy and Psychoeducation/Relaxation Training for Child Obsessive-Compulsive Disorder." *Journal of the American Academy of Child and Adolescent Psychiatry* 50: 1149–1161.

Reardon, L. E., E. W. Leen-Feldner, and C. Hayward. 2009. "A Critical Review of the Empirical Literature on the Relation Between Anxiety and Puberty." *Clinical Psychology Review* 29:1–23.

Sandberg, Sheryl. 2013. *Lean In: Women, Work, and the Will to Lead.* New York: Alfred A. Knopf.

Schwartz, C. E., N. Snidman, and J. Kagan. 1999. "Adolescent Social Anxiety as an Outcome of Inhibited Behavior in Childhood." *Journal of the American Academy of Child and Adolescent Psychiatry* 38:1008–1015.

Silverman, W. K., and W. M. Kurtines. 1996. *Anxiety and Phobic Disorders: A Pragmatic Approach.* New York: Plenum Press.

Stravynski, A., and D. Amado. 2001. "Social Phobia as a Deficit in Social Skills." In *From Social Anxiety to Social Phobia: Multiple Perspectives*, edited by S. G. Hofmann and P. M. DiBartolo. Boston: Allyn & Bacon.

Storch, E. A., G. R. Geffken, L. J. Merlo, M. L. Jacob, T. K. Murphy, T. K. Goodman, M. J. Larson, M. Fernandez, and K. Grabill. 2007. "Family Accommodation in Pediatric Obsessive-Compulsive Disorder." *Journal of Clinical Child and Adolescent Psychology* 36:207–216.

Suveg, C., and J. Zeman. 2004. "Emotion Regulation in Children with Anxiety Disorders." *Journal of Clinical Child and Adolescent Psychology* 33:750–759.

Swendsen, J., K. Conway, L. Degenhardt, M. Glantz, R. Jin, K. R. Merikangas, N. Sampson, and R. C. Kessler. 2010. "Mental Disorders as Risk Factors for Substance Use, Abuse and Dependence. Results from the 10-year Follow-up of the National Comorbidity Survey." *Addiction* 105:1117–1128.

Turner, S. M., D. C. Beidel, and R. M. Townsley. 1990. "Social Phobia: Relationship to Shyness." *Behaviour Research and Therapy* 28:497–505.

Van Oort, F. V. A., K. Greaves-Lord, F. C. Verhulst, J. Ormel, and A. C. Huizink. 2009. "The Developmental Course of Anxiety Symptoms During Adolescence: The TRAILS Study." *Journal of Child Psychology and Psychiatry* 50:1209–1217.

Wegner, D. M. 1994. "The Ironic Processes of Mental Control." *Psychological Review* 101: 34–52.

Wittchen, H. U., M. Stein, and R. Kessler. 1999. "Social Fears and Social Phobia in a Community Sample of Adolescents and Young Adults: Prevalence, Risk Factors, and Comorbidity." *Psychological Medicine* 29:309–323.

Woodward, L. J., and D. M. Fergusson. 2001. "Life Course Outcomes of Young People with Anxiety Disorders in Adolescence." *Journal of the American Academy of Child and Adolescent Psychiatry* 40:1086–1093.

Zill, N., D. Morrison, and M. Coiro. 1993. "Long-Term Effects of Parental Divorce on Parent-Child Relationships, Adjustment, and Achievement in Young Adulthood." *Journal of Family Psychology* 7:91–103.

Sheila Achar Josephs, PhD, is a clinical psychologist and anxiety expert with over twenty years of experience helping kids, teens, families, and adults. She is founder of Princeton Cognitive Therapy, a practice specializing in cognitive behavioral therapy (CBT) for anxiety. She has helped numerous kids, teens, parents, clinicians, and school professionals learn cutting-edge strategies to overcome anxiety. She also enjoys presenting workshops on teen stress and resilience for parents. To find out more, visit www.princetoncognitivetherapy.com.

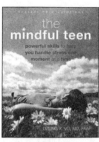

Register your **new harbinger** titles for additional benefits!

When you register your **new harbinger** title—purchased in any format, from any source—you get access to benefits like the following:

- Downloadable accessories like printable worksheets and extra content
- Instructional videos and audio files
- Information about updates, corrections, and new editions

Not every title has accessories, but we're adding new material all the time.

Access free accessories in 3 easy steps:

1. Sign in at NewHarbinger.com (or **register** to create an account).

2. Click on **register a book**. Search for your title and click the **register** button when it appears.

3. Click on the **book cover or title** to go to its details page. Click on **accessories** to view and access files.

That's all there is to it!

If you need help, visit:

NewHarbinger.com/accessories

new harbinger
CELEBRATING
40 YEARS